Beginners' Guide to
Water Gardening

Beginners' Guide to
Water Gardening
Graham Clarke

GUILD OF MASTER CRAFTSMAN PUBLICATIONS

First published 2002 by
Guild of Master Craftsman Publications Ltd,
166 High Street, Lewes,
East Sussex BN7 1XU

Reprinted 2003

ISBN 1 86108 243 6

British Cataloguing in Publication Data
A catalogue record of this book is available from the British Library.

Book design by Andy Harrison

Typeface: Meridien Roman

Colour origination by Viscan Graphics - Singapore

Printed and bound by CT Printing Ltd (Hong Kong)

The publishers are grateful to the following individuals and organisations who have kindly allowed us to reproduce their photographs in this book:

Harry Smith Photographic Collection: pp. 47, 57, 65 top, 67 right, 68 right, 69, 70, 76–77, 81, 85, 88, 143, 164–5.

Brian Bevan: pp. 13, 53, 56, 58, 61, 83, 89, 93, 122, 136–7, 144 bottom, 145 right, 160.
Michael Edwards: pp. 134 (x 2). **Tracy Hallett:** p. 95. **Pat Culling:** p. 132. **Melanie Mines:** p. 161

Harcostar: p. 9 centre. **Heissner:** p. 28. **Hozelock Cyprio:** pp. 14–17, 23 bottom, 29 bottom, 30 top, 31 right, (5), 40 bottom, 41 (2), 45. **Lotus:** p. 9 bottom. **Tetra:** p. 33 (7). **Trident:** p. 142. **Rapitest:** p. 43 bottom.

GMC/Anthony Bailey: pp. 20 left, 20 right, 21 (2), 22 (2), 23 top, 32, 49, 118 left, 120.
GMC/Ed Gabriel: front and back cover (4), pp. iii, 4, 7–8, 9 top, 11, 18, 24, 25 bottom, 27, 29 top, 30 bottom, 35, 38, 40 top, 43 top, 50, 140, 154, 158, 162–3. **GMC/Mark Baker:** pp. 15 top, 138 (2), 139 centre. **GMC/Martin Page:** pp. 55, 59, 63–4, 65 bottom, 66, 67 top left, 67 bottom left, 71–3, 75 top, 75 bottom, 79–80, 82, 84, 86–7, 90, 97, 101, 102 top left, 102 bottom left, 103, 105, 106 left, 106 right, 108 top, 108 bottom, 109–111, 112 middle left, 112 bottom left, 112 right, 113, 115, 117 (2), 118 right, 119, 121, 150, 155, 157 bottom. **GMC/Christine Richardson:** pp. 96 (2), 116 right, 148. **GMC/Chris Skarbon:** p. 25 top.

The author: pp. 6, 10, 12, 26 (2), 30 right, 34, 36–37, 48, 52, 60, 62, 68 left, 74, 78, 98 (2), 99, 100, 102 right, 104, 112 top left, 114, 116 left, 124–6, 135, 144 top, 146 (2), 147, 149, 151 (2), 152–3, 156 (2), 157 top,

The author would like to thank **Freda Cox** for her amazing illustrations (pp. 1, 2 and 3), **Michael Munday** for his charismatic fish (pp. 126–130), and **Rob Wheele** for his enchanting newts (pp. 138–9).

**In addition the publishers would like to thank
Merebrook Water Plants for their help.**

CONTENTS

NOTES

A NOTE ABOUT SEASONS

For the benefit of readers in both hemispheres, seasons – rather than months – are referred to throughout this book. This table shows the approximate month for each season:

NORTHERN HEMISPHERE			SOUTHERN HEMISPHERE
Early winter	= January	=	Early summer
Mid-winter	= February	=	Mid-summer
Late winter	= March	=	Late summer
Early spring	= April	=	Early autumn
Mid-spring	= May	=	Mid-autumn
Late spring	= June	=	Late autumn
Early summer	= July	=	Early winter
Mid-summer	= August	=	Mid-winter
Late summer	= September	=	Late winter
Early autumn	= October	=	Early spring
Mid-autumn	= November	=	Mid-spring
Late autumn	= December	=	Late spring

THE NAMING OF PLANTS

Plants may be known by their common names but they are classified by their Latin (or botanical) names. Each plant is classified by at least two words.

The genus, or first name, refers to a group of plants with similar botanical features. For example: hemerocallis, which is the Latin name for the day lily. The species, or second name, is a descriptive name for the plant, so *Hemerocallis multiflora* describes a very floriferous day lily.

Sometimes you will see a cross between the names. This refers to an interspecific hybrid which is the result of crossing two related species within the same genus. For example: *Astilbe × arendsii*, which is a cross between two different astilbes and has larger plumes.

A cultivar is produced by plant breeding and may result, for example, in different coloured or larger flowers, disease resistance or variegated foliage. This is written after the species and is not in Latin. For example: *Rheum palmatum* 'Atrosanguineum', which has deep red leaves. When the cultivar is particularly distinct and further removed from the original species, it is used straight after the genus. For example: *Nymphaea* 'Paul Hariot'.

A slight variation in the species which occurs naturally is termed a variety. For example: *Nuphar japonica* var. *variegata*, which has variegated leaves instead of the usual green.

POND SIZES

Throughout this book I have referred to the sizes of ponds as small, medium or large. Remembering that one gardener's small pond may be another's large lake, I think it worth mentioning that I have assumed the following approximate dimensions: small ponds are up to 2.2m^2 (22 sq ft) in area; medium ponds are between this and 5.25m^2 (55 sq ft) in area; large ponds have an area greater than this.

The depth of a pond becomes relevant where certain plants (or fish) are concerned, and so specific depths are referred to throughout the text.

INTRODUCTION

The first decorative gardens were built in ancient Egypt and evidence shows that water has been used as an ornamental feature, as well as for the more obvious use of irrigation of crops, virtually since the beginning of recorded history.

The Egyptians dammed water to irrigate the meagre crops growing in the hot inhospitable soils, as well as to prevent and reduce the impact of the frequent flooding of the Nile. Terraces and sluices played a part, as well as man-made channels, canals and reservoirs. Man was, for the first time, engineering the use of water.

The earliest gardeners soon recognized the potential of water as both a symbolic and decorative element, and it rapidly became a

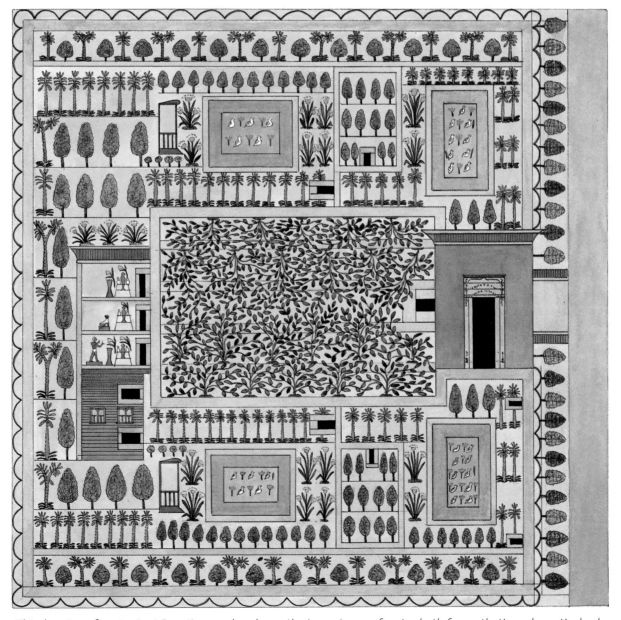

This drawing of an Ancient Egyptian garden shows the importance of water, both for aesthetic and practical value

feature of their gardens. What evidence do we have of this? Well, one example is that of the figurative sculpture, found by historians in Mesopotamia, and dated at around 4000 years old. It appears to have been used as a fountain, and so could be considered to be the prototype of today's ornamental garden fountains.

Another example took place around 3000 years ago during China's Shang dynasty, when gardens and parks incorporating water were created. The Yin-Yang symbol – the two opposing forces of life – were represented by water and rock.

And 2500 years ago Islamic garden 'designers' used two intersecting canals to create a geometric garden, representing the four rivers of paradise and the elements of water, fire, air and earth.

Much has been documented about the history of water in our lives, and how it is the essential provider of life. It is just as important today, of course, but in these chaotic modern times of fast living, fast food and fast cars, water is also seen as a facilitator of peace and harmony. Think of the tranquility of either a great lake or a meandering stream. Hundreds of thousands of people take their annual vacations to visit such places, to recharge their batteries, take in the clean air and to attempt to become at one with Nature.

Many of us try to recreate a little bit of this tranquility in our own gardens,

albeit on a much-reduced scale, and for most of us the appeal of a garden pond (or some such water feature) comes down to two things: first, it is an indisputable combination of beauty and serenity – two qualities that are hard to distinguish between and, for me, the one goes very much with the other.

Second, all water gardeners, no matter how 'devout', are fascinated to discover and encourage the secret hidden world that is teeming with life and interest down amongst the depths. Yes, water gardening is as much about enjoying another world, as it is about looking after fish and choosing waterlilies.

There are the more specific attributes, too, which make ponds enjoyable: the first has to be moving water – to many gardeners, the most enjoyable aspect of their pond is the sight and sound of a waterfall or fountain. Then there is the 'livestock' element, fish and assorted wildlife, which can become a near obsession to some pond owners.

My aim in this book is to point out to newcomers (and to remind the longer-serving water gardeners amongst us) that there are many facets to a pond. Some are rules to stick by, and others are ideas to copy. But all make very good sense, and most (if not all) are within anyone's capabilities.

LEFT: *An artist's impression of the 4000-year-old stone sculpture, thought to have been used as a fountain*

RIGHT: *An illustration depicting* The Garden of Fidelity, *commissioned in memory of Babur (1483–1530), founder of the Mogul Empire. Water is clearly the most important feature*

FIRST DECISIONS

Once you have decided to add a water feature to your garden, try to resist the temptation to rush out immediately and build it: unless you plan carefully, you could create all sorts of problems for the future. A good feature takes time to install, as well as a considerable amount of money and, once *in situ*, it cannot be moved easily. So don't risk spoiling your enjoyment of the garden and the feature itself – make sure you first consider every option fully.

When incorporating water into your garden for the first time, you can treat the garden as a blank canvas and choose where the feature will go, as well as its style and size. But remember, there are four limiting factors:

● The type of garden you have: a magnificently opulent fountain would be completely out of place in an informal garden.

● Your garden's proportions: these should determine the size of the feature.

● The size of your budget: this speaks for itself.

● The level of your enthusiasm: how thoroughly you plan and execute your ideas can make all the difference to the success of your plan.

A straight-edged formal pond looks impressive, especially when sited near the house

WHAT DESIGN? WHAT STYLE?

Water is versatile and adaptable and can be incorporated in many forms. Small features might include a barrel pond or cobblestone fountain, either of which would be ideal for a tiny town garden or patio area. Ponds, perhaps 1–2m (3–6ft) across, are what most gardeners possess, and these can be wonderful to create and nurture. At the other end of the scale you might consider a lake or large bog garden – if there is the room.

Formal designs

These are either circular, oval, or angular – a square, rectangle or other geometric shape. Formal ponds are particularly suitable where space is limited. They look best in more formal surroundings, for example near the house, or in conjunction with other features such as straight paths and patios. Raised or sunken ponds can add a further attractive dimension to the garden.

Informal designs

By contrast, informal ponds are irregular in shape, with soft, sweeping curves and few, if any, straight lines or sharp angles. This type of design is best suited to a garden planted in a relaxed way – a sort of cottage garden, with flowers of all sizes and colours. If you like lots of plants, an informal style of pond would suit you best. For example, a bog garden can be created as an extension of the pond, making a perfect transition between the pond and garden.

Still-water pond

This is the basic, unsophisticated type of pond, without a fountain or waterfall, and no

A water feature, such as this pump and bath, will provide sound and movement in the garden

mechanical filtration using pumps. This may sound rather boring, yet in many cases it is preferable if you wish to keep fish and grow a variety of aquatic plants – especially waterlilies, which hate too much moving water around their stems and leaves.

Moving water pond

For most of us, the perfect pond is one in which there is some form of moving water. It may be the trickle of a little fountain, or a big gusher with a larger water feature; a gentle cascade over some rocks or, at the other end of the scale, a waterfall torrent. In all cases, unless your garden contains a natural waterfall, or you live on a geyser, the water will be recycled using a pump.

Fish pond

There are two fixed rules about keeping fish in an outdoor pond:

Facts & Figures 1

Wherever it is sited, and whatever style you choose, your pond should be 45cm (18in) or more deep at some point, to prevent the water freezing completely in winter. If the surface area is 2.4m² (50 sq ft) or more, and if you plan to have various types of fish, then a depth of 60cm (2ft) is better. For even larger ponds, a depth of 75cm (30in) is desirable.

Patio ponds are often raised, so you can sit on the side and see the water up close

Facts & Figures 2

For a 'proper' pond, which can be expected to stay clear, you should aim for a water surface of at least 2.1m² (40 sq ft). Planting a third of the pond surface will create the best ecological balance.

1. *The dimensions of the pond – or more accurately, the volume of water in the pond – should determine the amount and size of the fish introduced.*

2. *The types of fish kept must be fully hardy and not 'tender exotics', which would come to harm during a cold winter.*

'Mixed pond' would be a more appropriate name than 'fish pond' for, although you would be keeping a selection of fish in it, there would undoubtedly be plants and pondweed, inevitably there would be insect life and very probably amphibians such as toads, frogs and newts. However, regardless of the eventual constituent parts of your pond, it is the keeping of fish which many gardeners enjoy. The colours, the timidity and the serenity that fish bring to the scene cannot be equalled.

Wildlife pond

I conducted a survey with readers of a national gardening magazine a few years ago, and 86% maintained that their main reason for having a pond was to watch and encourage wildlife. Informal ponds make the best environments for aquatic wildlife, too. In theory, a true wildlife pond would be one that was built entirely from natural materials and contained only plants and animals native to the area. In reality, however, these preconditions are either difficult or impossible to recreate and so most wildlife ponds are artificial havens. And havens they are, for the hundreds of species which will be attracted to the pond will themselves attract other non-aquatic animals, such as birds, bees, butterflies and foxes.

Raised pond

Any raised feature in an otherwise flat garden will add interest, but one containing water is always special. Patio ponds are often raised, so you can sit on the edge and appreciate the pond life at close quarters. It may also be the only way of having a pond if the ground cannot be excavated. If a very deep pond is required – e.g. for keeping koi – then elevating it would mean less excavation and reduce the overall costs, which could otherwise be huge. A raised pond can also be a disincentive to marauding creatures – predominately cats and herons – which can mercilessly decimate a collection of fish.

Facts & Figures 3

The minimum safe distance between a tree and a pond is that equivalent to the height of the tree in question.

A small, raised water feature, including fountain

A half-barrel water feature with an old-fashioned water pump

This purpose-made tray and water urn are almost small enough to be used indoors

Wooden decking can provide an excellent edging to a pond and is more comfortable underfoot than paving

Container features

Small water features which do not require an actual pond were once rare to see; today they sell in their millions and can be bought as manufactured items, or made up at home with paraphernalia accrued from all manner of sources. As long as the end result is watertight, your imagination can run riot!

A small water feature can be anything from a wall-mounted ornate reservoir, that is little more than a glorified bird bath, through to wooden barrels, Japanese bamboo bird and deer scarers and old kitchen sinks, to more sophisticated pebble and millstone fountains. These can be fairly inexpensive, quick to install, stunning to look at and a marvellous talking point. On the downside, the small size will limit the range of fish or plants you can keep in it; shade will be required for part of the day in very hot weather, to prevent the water temperature rising to dangerous levels for the water life, and regular checks will be needed to replenish water levels.

Facts & Figures 4

When laying flexible liners, it is always better to stick to gentle curves and simple shapes. Avoid sharp corners and fussiness. Both gently sloping and straight vertical sides can also cause problems, so it is better to aim for 20° sides.

Conclusion

Whatever design and style you choose for your pond, avoid having too many niches, nooks and crannies, otherwise it could be a real problem to construct and look over-fussy when completed. When in doubt, always choose the simple option, as straightforward, uncomplicated shapes are

Do not bring the lawn right to the water's edge – the grass will be difficult to cut

usually more attractive than over-ambitious, complex designs.

THE POND SURROUND

In many cases, the pond surround is just as important to the overall appearance of the garden as the pond itself and it is important to plan the surround at the same time as the pond, otherwise the end result could be at best incongruous, and at worst, hideous. There are many styles of pond surround available, and I list a few of them below:

Wooden decking

Gardeners have been a little slow to adopt the largely American, Scandinavian and Far Eastern ideas of surrounding a pond with wooden decking. But, in recent years, dozens of manufacturers have emerged to make this a popular and affordable garden feature. Decking is warmer and more comfortable underfoot than traditional paving, blends well with the garden, and is more sympathetic to the concept of the garden being a 'living space' – the fabled 'outdoor room', or 'extension of the home'.

Rock and paving

Natural and/or artificial stone can make ideal partners for a pond, whether as paving around the edge, walling to form the sides, or rock and stone to form the water feature itself. Natural quarried stone is ideal for many gardens – particularly if you want your feature to be sympathetic to the local environment – but most, particularly real slate, can be extremely expensive to buy. Artificial paving and walling (which is mostly concrete) can look very realistic, is cheaper and often simpler to lay.

Beds and borders

These are, arguably, as natural-looking as any other style of pond surround. Plants growing over and into the water can be most appealing, especially with wildlife ponds and bog gardens, where there is often no defining line between the water and the planted areas. The key here is to allow access points at strategic places around the pond's edge, so you can get close to the water.

Lawns

The least natural, and most frustrating pond surround of all is an area of maintained lawn. It is least natural because it doesn't occur in the wild – grass banks may run down to highland streams, but the grass is not maintained in an ornamental sense. I use the word 'frustrating', because, if you do cut grass close to a pond, you cannot avoid getting clippings onto the water surface.

Facts & Figures 5

When digging a hole for your pond, you can make it any shape you want, but calculating the amount of liner required becomes a nightmare, so use this simple formula:

Length of sheet required = pond length, plus 2 x pond depth, plus an extra 60cm (2ft)

Width of sheet required = pond width, plus 2 x pond depth, plus an extra 60cm (2ft)

WHERE TO SITE YOUR FEATURE?

There are five golden rules for siting a pond:
● Choose a sunny spot, preferably sheltered from cold easterly winds. For a pond to reach its full potential in a temperate climate, for instance, it should be positioned where the sun can shine upon it for at least half the day – indeed waterlilies will only give of their best if they receive six hours or more of sunshine per day. It has to be said, however, that in very hot countries – such as the Mediterranean and north Africa – some shade is positively beneficial!
● Avoid overhanging trees – they cast shade, and their fallen leaves will readily pollute the water with harmful salts and gases, which also encourage algae. The worst offenders are horse chestnut, laburnum, holly and – would you believe – willow, so avoid these trees if you can. Plums and cherries, meanwhile, host waterlily aphids in winter.
● Make sure your site is level. This makes for easier installation, a better-looking result, and will be easier to maintain.
● Choose a low-lying site, to avoid unnecessary exposure to the elements, but make sure that your chosen location is above the water table, otherwise flooding will be a regular occurrence.
● Do not place a pond at the base of a slope. Run-off from the higher levels will cause problems, and places like this also act as 'frost pockets' because the average temperature of this part of the garden is lower, and so water will more readily ice over.

The following are merely recommendations for the best siting of a pond, not preconditions, like those listed above:

If a pond is big enough for plants or fish, chances are it is also big enough for a child to fall in

● Site the pond close to the house and power supplies (for running the electric pumps, filters, under-water lighting, and so on).
● Ensure that the pond is clearly visible from several vantage points around the garden.
● Avoid locations with unsightly surroundings, especially those that would cast ugly reflections in the water.

WHICH MATERIALS?

Ponds need to be watertight and, within reason, it doesn't matter how you achieve this. Today there are three main options:

● Prefabricated ponds
Rigid moulded liners made from vacuum-formed plastic are the cheapest and they usually come with built-in shelves. They are relatively easy to install, and many people like them because the shape is predetermined, but they are fairly short-lived. PVC-based and rubberized compounds are available; these are slightly more expensive, but are longer lasting. Moulded fibreglass pre-formed liners are the longest lasting of all, but are not so easy to find, and are more expensive when you do.

● Flexible liners
These are basically lengths of waterproof sheeting, enabling you to build a pond of any shape or size. More planning is required, and calculating the

---

Facts & Figures 6

Use this guide to help you select the right thickness of liner.

Ponds under 10m² (30 sq ft): 0.5mm liner

Ponds up to 15cm (6in) depth: 1mm liner

Ponds over 15cm (6in) depth: 1.5mm liner

amount of liner you need is not always easy, (see Facts & Figures Tip 5, on page 11). Lined ponds are ideal for informal schemes, since the sheeting will fit most shapes and contours, albeit with varying amounts of creasing. Many raised ponds, which at first appear to be constructed entirely of bricks and cement, are actually lined inside. The best reliability comes with rubber sheeting known as butyl, but PVC and LDPE (low-density polyethylene) sheets are also to be recommended. Buy lengths with a guarantee of 20 years or more. Polythene is common at the cheaper end of the scale, but it lacks pliability and becomes brittle after prolonged exposure to sunlight, so is best avoided. Finally there are 'geotextile' liners, which are rubber-based liners impregnated with sodium bentonite. These are self-healing liners – if they sustain a minor puncture, the bentonite will plug the hole.

● Concrete ponds

Concrete was the main choice years ago, but is no longer favoured because making a satisfactory concrete pond takes a great deal of skill, time and hard labour. Achieving the right mix, applying it correctly and keeping it workable, are tasks that many beginners get badly wrong. Yet, properly designed and constructed, a concrete pond can be elegant and have an air of permanence unequalled by other materials.

BETTER TO BE SAFE THAN SORRY

Safety must be paramount at all times, as any water feature is a potential hazard. If a pond is big enough for plants and fish, chances are it is also big enough for a child to fall in. So safety must be a major consideration if children are likely to be present. Choose a site with all-round visibility, so that you can keep an eye on children while they are playing in the vicinity.

Barrier fencing is an obvious safety measure, and it need not be unsightly. Picket fencing is certainly an effective barrier (and can look quite attractive, too) but it must be at least 75cm (30in) high. If end posts are slotted into sockets at ground level it need not be a permanent fixture. Both metal hoop fencing as used in parks, and chain link fencing as used around school playgrounds, will merge into the background

> ### Facts & Figures 7
> Herons will gobble up a pond's stock of fish if given the chance, but these crane-like birds will also eat small mammals, reptiles, insects, worms and even small birds. Dawn and dusk are the favoured times for eating.

greenery and be less obtrusive if painted dark green. Heavy grilles placed over the pond might save lighter children from taking a dip, but this is hardly an attractive element for a garden pool.

The barriers mentioned above will also protect your fish from cats and herons – the two main enemies of the outdoor fish keeper. But as far as children are concerned, to be honest, if your pond poses a permanent risk to them, it is better to be without it until they reach an age when you do not have to watch them constantly.

Herons tend to visit garden ponds – and do their damage – at dawn or dusk

CHAPTER 2

HOW TO START

There are, of course, many ways of featuring water in a garden so it is crucial to establish at the outset the type of feature that you want. Essentially there are three general types:

1. *Feature with moving water (fountain, cascade, stream)*
2. *Still pond for fish and wildlife (and plants)*
3. *Self-contained water 'container' (barrel, wall fountain, raised pond)*

Pre-formed waterfall header

Whichever feature you choose, consider very carefully how best it can be designed into the context of your garden so that it feels and looks right. In this way you will ensure that the feature – and therefore the whole garden – is pleasing aesthetically.

Firstly, decide on the mood or style of your feature, and how it will look as part of the overall garden: it could, for instance, be informal, with curving sides and associated planting to make a natural setting. Or, it could be very formal, comprising a water feature with lots of straight edges and very little planting.

COMMITTING TO PAPER

If you are planning a feature that is more complex than a simple hole in the ground filled with water, then it would be wise to produce a scale drawing or plan of the area. This must include all of the garden's 'fixtures and fittings', i.e. the house, greenhouse/shed, immovable and desirable trees and shrubs, paths/driveways, paving and walling, drains and sewers, electricity poles, and so on. Consider also whether you might want to extend your home at some stage in the future; it would be a shame and a great waste of time, effort and money, to install a major water feature only to dig it out eighteen months later when an extension is built.

It is tempting to try to minimize the overall effort when designing a water feature, but it may be necessary to alter or move fixtures to

Cross section of a small pond and fountain

Similar pond with pump and circulating cascade

accommodate it, so don't compromise the garden just to save on effort. If the pond really needs to go where the greenhouse is currently sited, and there is somewhere else for the greenhouse to go, then do it.

The best way to start a paper plan is to conduct your own 'survey' of the garden. Walk around the house (and any fixed outbuildings) and make a large sketch of the layout, in plan form but not necessarily to scale.

A long, flexible measuring tape is useful, and a good starting point is a particular part of the house, say the back door. Measure the distance from the door to your proposed water feature. This gives you a mental picture of distance combined with an actual measurement.

One stage further would be to prepare several plans, each incorporating a pond of a different shape and size, located at different points within your general garden scheme, but always in accordance with the rules of where not to site a pond, as set out in the last chapter. If you don't want to prepare a new garden plan for each design, simply produce one and then move cut-outs of different shaped and sized ponds within the layout until you are happy with a particular grouping. Alternatively, if you have access to a computer there are a number of excellent garden design software packages that will offer you much versatility in drafting a plan.

The final act, prior to acquisition and construction, is to lay a hosepipe on the ground to form the outline of your proposed pond site. Few people bother to do this, but it can resolve a number of issues and avoid future regrets. Live with this for a few days. You will then be able to

Avoid placing a pond under overhanging trees

make adjustments, and satisfy yourself that this is absolutely the best place, the best size and the best shape for your water feature.

EXCAVATION AND INSTALLATION

The first thing that any gardener planning to reconstruct a garden should be aware of, particularly if they are undertaking much of the construction work themselves, is that the whole project should be fun.

If you are planning to employ professional landscapers or builders to do the 'heavy' part of

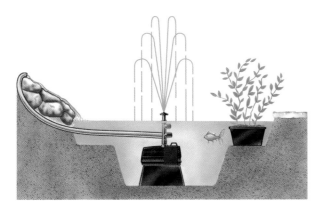

Some pumps can run fountains and cascades together

Cross section of a small pebble fountain

Facts & Figures 8

Any drawn plan of your proposed water feature must be large enough to accommodate all of the 'fixtures' within 6m (20ft) of it.

your garden construction it is always important to get several estimates for work to be carried out. Professionals are likely to work outside in all weathers but, if you're doing it yourself, you have the luxury of picking and choosing when to do the work.

Nobody really likes the idea of their garden turning into a building site but, if the job involves a lot of concrete work, such as the building of walls and patios – or even that of the pond itself – then it is probably inevitable.

Site clearance is, arguably, the most fundamental aspect to garden reconstruction. It may involve simply shouting at the dog to get out of the way, or it might require a degree of demolition, lifting and disposal of slabs and the hiring of the ubiquitous skip (this latter operation can be quite costly, so only hire one when there is a genuine need).

The trees that you want to keep can hardly be called obstacles, but in some ways that is what they are. These would normally include trees over 5m (15ft) high which, unless they are diseased or dangerous, are not worth felling. In addition, be aware of hidden obstacles, such as well-heads, drains and drainage pipes, manhole covers, electric cabling and assorted lumps of concrete hidden just under the soil.

With your plan firmly in hand you, or the landscapers, will need to mark out the site and it is crucial to know exactly where any walls are to be built and paths laid. Even a few inches out in any direction can cause big problems (especially with more intricate designs).

Thin lines of white spray paint can be used to mark bare soil and pegs, and taut string can be employed to indicate heights of walls and eventual paths. A good, old-fashioned spade should be used to mark out shallow trenches for such things as the water feature.

Installing a prefabricated pond

With this type of pond, the excavation of the hole into which the prefabricated unit will sit is crucial. If your chosen pond is a regular or symmetrically shaped unit (square, circle, rectangle, oval, etc), turn the unit upside down, and position it directly over the precise place you want the finished pond to be. Depending on the shape and size of the unit, this may or may not be a two-person job. With a stick, spade, or handfuls of sand, mark an outline right around the rim of the unit, but bring the mark out from the edge by about 15cm (6in). This extra space will allow for miscalculations in digging and, just as importantly, will permit backfilling later with soft soil or sand.

If your chosen pond is informal rather than symmetrical (such as the most popular kidney-shaped style), then upturning and marking out as described above will not work. Instead, place the unit upright over its intended position, and level it out with supports. Insert vertical stakes or canes

Many manufacturers make and supply a range of pre-formed ponds to meet the needs of most first-time water gardeners

Facts & Figures 9

When backfilling the sides of a prefabricated pond during installation, match the height of the backfilled soil or sand with the height and level of the water filling the inside of the pond. This prevents buckling of the side walls.

in the ground at intervals all the way around, then remove the unit, and measure the depth and size of any shelves that are moulded in to it. Now with your spade, dig a level, flat-bottomed hole as marked out, but only dig to a depth just a little deeper than the level of the first shelf. Rake over the bottom of the hole and then stand the pond unit inside the hole and press down so that when you remove it again, you will see that the deeper section of the unit has left an impression.

Remove the unit again and excavate the newly marked section down to about 10cm (4in) below where the bottom of the pond will be. Always check that the pond is sitting horizontally by using a straight-edged board and a spirit level. Check in six or seven directions, to ensure that the hole is being dug with a level base. There is nothing worse than a lopsided pond and water will always find its level, even when the pond is not, making it look unsightly.

Now check the hole thoroughly, removing any large or sharp stones. Compact the soil, and then spread a 5cm (2in) layer of builders' sand on to the base. Lower the pond gently into position, and add or take away sand until you are happy with the level. Keep checking with the spirit level. If you have measured correctly, the lip of the pond should end up lying just below ground level.

Next comes the satisfying bit – running water into the unit for the first time. But don't fill the whole pond. Run just a few inches into the bottom to stabilize the unit, and to bed the bottom of it on to the sand base. Then fill in some of the larger gaps around the edge of the pond unit with sieved soil or builder's sand. To backfill, pour the sand or soil into the space and then ram it down with a large piece of wood. This will help to ensure that there are no air pockets.

Add more water and backfill as you go. By doing the filling and backfilling at the same time,

you are exerting even pressure on to the sides of the unit – front and back – and so avoiding buckling of the walls.

Fill to about 10cm (4in) from the lip of the pond. This will allow you room to complete your job, which may be to plant perennials or bog plants along the edge of the pond, or to lay paving stones.

Installing a lined pond

Before you dig the hole for the pond, go around the outside of the proposed pond site, removing a thin layer of turf or topsoil, about 45cm (18in) wide, with a spade. This strip will eventually form the edge of the pond, onto which the flexible liner will overlap, and over which the pond edging – paving slabs, bricks, etc – will be placed.

Dig the rest of the hole. With this type of pond the sides can slope to almost any angle from 70° to 0° (i.e. a gently sloping pond or home-made 'beach'). The shallower the slope, the better it is for wildlife. Shape the shelves as you dig down, allowing enough width – 30cm (12in) minimum – for standing planted aquatic baskets.

If your soil is very sandy or loose, it is advisable to install a supporting back wall to the top shelf, to prevent damage to the edge once the pond is in use. This can be done by lining the back of the shelf with brick or building blocks and cementing them in place.

As excavation proceeds, keep checking with a spirit level to ensure that the shelves are horizontal. Unless you want to place planted

Pond liners are available in rolls or pre-cut packs – some even come with a 30-year guarantee

containers there, it is not so important for the bottom of the pond to be absolutely level.

Before laying the butyl or rubber liner, you should provide an 'underlay', e.g. a layer of builders' sand some 5cm (2in) thick, so the excavation should be deeper by this amount to accommodate it. Pre-made underlays consist of strips of old carpet, or proprietary underlay felt; with either of these, the thicknesses are so small, your excavation will not need to be adjusted to accommodate them.

Remove any sharp stones or boulders and position the underlay. If you are using sand, dampen it so that it stays in place. If you are using carpet or felt, press it down firmly. It is especially important to run this underlay over any sharp corners, such as that caused by a reinforced back wall of bricks or blocks.

Installing the liner is not difficult. The easiest way is to mould the liner into the excavation, smoothing out as many creases as you can. Then run a hose into the deepest part, adjusting any folds that occur as it fills.

Once the pond is full, trim the edges of the liner, leaving sufficient width all round to form a good overlap – this will eventually be covered by the edging or surround of your choice.

Constructing a concrete pond

A lot of fairly strenuous work is involved in creating a pond in concrete. You will need to mix the sand and cement and then transport barrowsful of the stuff to and fro. It also takes weeks to construct a concrete pond, rather than a mere day or two as for the alternative methods. What makes concrete a realistic option however is its longevity: if made well, it will almost certainly outlast either rigid or flexible liner ponds.

Begin by marking out and digging the hole, making it about 15cm (6in) deeper and wider than the finished desired size. Shape any shelves and firm the surface of the soil so that there are few loose fragments. Ensure that the sides are no steeper than 45°, otherwise you will not be able to prevent the wet concrete from sliding to the bottom of the slope.

LEFT: Small water features such as this self-contained pebble fountain are ideal for small gardens

If your garden soil is heavy clay, you may have noticed that it becomes dry and cracked in the summer. It effectively 'shrinks'. It would not be good for the concrete to be in regular contact with a soil that expands and shrinks in this way, so you should line the hole with a 8cm (3in) layer of moist builders' sand. If you live on a sandy soil this stage can be ignored.

Next, line the hole with a 5cm (2in) thick base layer of concrete. Although it is possible to build the whole pond using one strength of concrete, a far stronger and more durable pond will be created if you adjust the ratios. Ideally, there should be three stages. The first stage – the base layer – should be mixed to the following recipe: seven parts 15mm ($^3/_4$in) gravel; three parts builders' sand; one part cement. Measure the ingredients dry, with a shovel or bucket.

Always mix the concrete as near to the pond site as possible, on a hard surface such as paving or a large board. The concrete consistency should be stiff, but moist. Weak joints may be created if you add a new layer to a previous layer that has not set properly, so plan to complete each layer in a day and allow it to harden and dry overnight.

Start by lining the hole with the base layer. An hour or so after you have finished the layer, use a stiff broom to brush the drying surface, and so create a rough key for the next layer. Leave to dry overnight.

Next day, cover the base layer with 5cm (2in) mesh wire netting. This will reinforce the concrete. Overlap the strips of wire by about 10cm (4in) and tread it into place, using your feet to mould it into the contours of the pond. Next, mix and lay another lining of concrete, but this time make it about 10cm (4in) thick, and make it to the following recipe: three parts 15mm ($^3/_4$in) gravel; two parts builders' sand; one part cement, plus optional waterproofing agent to bind the mixture together. Smooth the edges with a builder's trowel, protect the surface

Facts & Figures 10

Warm weather will make flexible liners more flexible and easier to handle. So, if possible, unroll the liner and leave it in the sun for about 30 minutes before using.

from strong sunlight (with sacking or horticultural fleece) and leave it to set for a couple of weeks. In really hot weather it is advisable to damp it down using a watering can.

Finally, spread a 5cm (2in) thick top layer over the whole area. This should be made to the following recipe: four parts builders' sand; one part cement, plus waterproofing agent. Leave to set for a couple of weeks.

Once the final layer of concrete has set hard, coat it with a waterproofing primer and sealant, and leave it to dry. Sweep the interior of the pond and flush out all debris prior to filling with water. This will also help initially to reduce the amount of lime in the water.

CONSTRUCTING WALLS

Many water features make use of walls. Raised ponds need low walls to support the weight and volume of water, and wall-mounted fountains (like the ubiquitous lion's head) speak for themselves.

Whichever type of wall you need there's no escaping the fact that what goes up, must go down! Good, deep foundations are the key to a robust wall and that means digging a trench at least 60cm (2ft) deep. This will allow for 45cm (18in) of concrete for the main foundation, and a further 15cm (6in) for the first course of bricks to remain below ground level.

Use wooden pegs hammered into the ground and a builder's line – or some string tied to sticks – to mark out the eventual position of the wall and use this as a guide to excavate the

foundations. The trench should be roughly twice as wide as the width of the wall it will support.

The foundation material is basically a concrete mix, poured in to the trench you have just dug. For small walls you can now get a ready-to-use powder that is poured dry into the trench and then packed down, smoothed off and watered. It will set rock hard within half an hour or so. It is probably not as strong as concrete, but significantly easier for smaller jobs.

For larger walls, the foundation mix should be concrete. Work an amount sufficient to fill a single wheelbarrow at a time, otherwise it may harden before you get around to using it all. Mix one part cement to six parts aggregate, ballast or sharp sand. Add little amounts of water gradually, until you reach a consistency similar to that of gloss paint – too much water will require you to add more cement/ballast and this can be wasteful.

Start pouring the mix in to the trench. If your new wall will adjoin an existing one, start from that end.

Use a spirit level and a bit of old wood with a straight edge to tamp down and flatten the concrete, so that the final level is at just the right height for the first course of bricks or blocks. The foundation mix will harden sufficiently overnight in summer, or over a couple of days in winter.

Brickwork

Most garden walls are built with modern lightweight Celcon or Toplite blocks. These are cheaper than bricks and have superseded breeze blocks, which are made from highly expensive,

A rotating concrete mixer can be hired relatively cheaply and saves a lot of time

Before digging for a concrete pond, or building walls, the site should be marked out

Facts & Figures 11

If a concrete pond has been well sealed, no toxins should leach out from the concrete. To be sure, use a pH test kit after filling the pond with water to check on its acidity/alkalinity levels. Over pH8.5 indicates a high lime content. Neutralize by adding potassium permanganate, which will initially turn the water a light pinkish colour, and leave for a few days. Pump the water out of the pond, rinse the sides and base thoroughly, refill with clean water and re-test. Leave for about six weeks before introducing any fish.

imported blown volcanic clay. Heavier and sturdier walls can be achieved with the use of 'concrete' blocks. These are, however, more difficult to cut and transport around the garden. If you're building a smaller wall, use ordinary bricks, which can be laid in small spaces, and won't need to be cut. Brick prices rise steeply with the better-made and designed display bricks.

Use pegs and a builder's line to mark out the position of the 'face' of the wall (the side of the wall that will be most visible); this should follow a straight line, unless there is a designed curve (see below right).

It's now time to start bricklaying. You can mix your mortar from one part cement to six parts soft sand, or buy a ready-made mix from a large

DIY store. Work one wheelbarrow load at a time and, if the weather is hot, cover the mix with a sheet of plastic or wood to stop the mortar from drying out too quickly.

Begin by trowelling a 1cm (½in) layer of mortar on to the footing. Then, using your line as a guide, and checking every so often with a spirit level, start bedding in the first course of bricks.

If the first brick is to butt up to an existing wall, then its ends will need to be 'buttered'. To do this, hold the brick in one hand, trowel on a small amount of mortar, and then roughly shape it so that the mortar is at its thickest in the middle, sloping off to both sides. Then lay the brick lengthways, with the buttered end touching the bricks of the wall. Tamp the brick down on to the mortar bed and check that the brick is lined up with a spirit level in 90° directions.

Lay brick after brick, course after course then, after about six courses, step back and start cleaning up the mortar, which should be stiff enough to work. First use a jointing iron, or the bend in a piece of 1cm (½in) copper pipe, to smooth a nice clean finish between each course, then brush off the small blobs of semi-dry mortar with a soft hand brush.

THE ELECTRICS

It is likely that you will want to run a fountain or a waterfall in your pond, or perhaps you'll want some garden lighting. With all of these you will need to supply power, and the whole subject of electricity and electrical safety must be treated

Wall foundations should be 45cm (18in) deep, with room for the first brick course to be underground

Ordinary bricks should be used for the bottom few courses, or for smaller walls

with great caution. There is an important difference between wiring inside the house and wiring anywhere in the garden. To begin with, the latter is much more likely to give you a shock. There are two reasons for this. The first is simply that garden electric wiring is much more likely to get damaged than wiring hidden inside the walls, floor or roof of a house. Classic examples are cutting through a flex with a hedge trimmer or lawnmower or digging into (and perhaps through) a buried cable with a sharp spade. The second reason why electricity is so dangerous outdoors – especially in and around a pond – is that it is invariably associated with water (or at least moisture) and, as we all know, water and electricity do not mix.

Let's be clear about the different safety measures which apply to electric wiring. The most familiar is probably fusing – but its function is to protect the wiring not you: in particular, fusing prevents wiring overheating and, possibly, causing a fire. A big fuse protects the whole house (and all the circuits); medium-sized fuses protect individual circuits; small fuses (for example, in a plug) protect the flex leading to electrical appliances and, sometimes, tiny fuses within an appliance protect its wiring.

What does help to protect you with appliances that have metal casings is 'earthing'. For example, a loose live wire inside could cause the casing to become live and so give you a shock. If an appliance is 'earthed', the metal casing is connected to the 'earth' wire in the plug so that if a live wire does touch it, a short circuit is caused;

this blows at least one of the fuses, thus protecting you from an electric shock. But this doesn't really apply in the garden, as outdoor electrical equipment is invariably non-earthed with a plastic non-electric current carrying casing – a method of protection called 'double insulation'.

Residual current devices (RCDs)

What makes electricity dangerous to you in the garden is that you could provide a perfect earth connection if you touch a live wire – particularly if you are standing on damp ground – and the short circuit that then passes through you could kill you.

This is where residual current protection comes in. A residual current device (RCD) monitors the currents flowing in the live and neutral wires of a flex or cable and acts like a switch to cut off the electrical supply if it detects even a tiny difference (perhaps because some of the current is trying to flow through you).

RCDs have saved the lives of people who have, for example, cut through the flex of a lawnmower – picking up the live severed flex could otherwise be fatal. It is obvious, therefore, that an RCD should ALWAYS be used with outside electrics.

The RCD can be in the plug used to wire an appliance, in an adaptor fitted between the plug and the socket, in the socket, on the circuit that supplies the garden, on all socket outlet circuits in the house and garden or protecting the whole house. Having a single RCD to protect the whole house sounds like the best idea, but it isn't: what is known as 'nuisance tripping' can mean that frozen food in a freezer can be ruined if the RCD

Build up the courses of bricks, but after six courses step back and clean up the mortar

Lightweight Celcon or Toplite blocks are cheaper than bricks and perfect for walls that are to be rendered

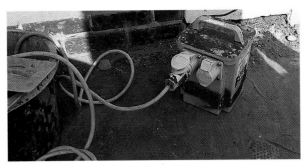

Home gardeners should always use RCDs for reasons of safety, but professional landscapers must use durable transformers

trips whilst you are on holiday; if you trip a whole-house RCD when using an appliance, all the lights will go out and you could be plunged into darkness.

Some water garden suppliers have RCDs in part of their range, whilst whole-house and circuit RCDs are also made by electrical accessory manufacturers. These are usually available from garden centres and DIY stores.

Low-voltage garden electric circuits

Much of the electric wiring you will have in or around your pond is likely to be low-voltage. That is, run at a safe 12 or 24 volts from a transformer. Only the transformer needs be connected to mains electricity; the low-voltage cable, which runs to the pond lights or to a low-voltage pond pump, can then be run along the surface of the ground without posing any danger. Legislation, and therefore manufacturers, err on the side of safety, and in many countries now electrical items such as pond lights have to be low-voltage: mains-voltage versions are no longer permitted. Some transformers are designed to be used outside and, if waterproof, even in the pond itself; if not, they must be used either inside the house or in a garden shed or other outbuilding with the low-voltage cable run outside. The problem that arises with a low-voltage circuit is how to run the cable from the

It is essential that all electrical junction boxes and connectors are waterproof, and made for outdoor use

house or other outbuilding and into the pond. The simplest way to get it out of the house, is to drill a hole in a convenient window frame, pass the cable through and then seal the hole with a matching silicone sealant or building mastic. To get it into the pond, you can simply pass it in behind some of the surrounding stones, or buy the special watertight cable lead-outs which some manufacturers make specifically for passing cable through walls.

Mains-voltage garden circuits

Serious pond owners will want to have a permanent outside electric circuit. Unless you are extremely competent, this should always be installed by a professional electrician. Such a circuit should have its cable buried in the ground deep enough to avoid being severed by digging with a spade, i.e. at least two spits deep. It is possible to use normal house wiring cable for this, but it must be protected by a rigid PVC conduit; the alternative is proper armoured cable, available through DIY stores and electrical retailers, which requires special fittings for the termination at either end. External sockets (also available through electrical wholesalers) have their own special plugs – each socket comes with a plug and extra plugs are available.

The alternative to a plug and socket, for permanent wiring, is a junction box with up to six outlets. These are widely available from water garden suppliers and can either be switched or unswitched (a separate switch serves each outlet).

Joining cable

If for any reason you need to join mains electric cable in the garden, you must make sure that you have the right type of connector, i.e. weatherproof or waterproof. The non-weatherproof kind is only suitable for use indoors and should not be considered for anything to do with the garden. You pay more for the weatherproof kind which can be used outside and even more for the watertight versions, some of which are suitable for immersion in a pond. Check the packaging and instructions carefully to make sure you get the type you require: all water garden centres should have suitable connectors as all the major suppliers have connectors in their range.

CHAPTER 3

ADDING FEATURES

The sound of moving water can even help to mask the noise of nearby traffic

Water that is moving, whether spurting, trickling, cascading or plummeting, is one of the great joys of pond-keeping. There are small contrivances such as spurting frogs, millstones, lions' heads and even peeing urchins. And then of course there are the larger features requiring the movement of a greater water volume, such as streams, waterfalls, 'hole-in-the-wall' falls, cascades and fountains.

In many cases, sound is as important as the visual effect. There is little doubt that the sound of moving water can appear to have a cooling effect on a hot patio, and some even claim that it can mask – or partly mask – the noise of traffic from a busy nearby road. But in order to 'move' water, we must invest in a pump or two (or more, if the volume of water to be moved, or the distances involved, are considerable).

The thought of a softly falling waterfall on a sunny day is hugely appealing, but there is an even more fundamental reason why it is a good idea to have a waterfall, fountain, or cascade and that is because it helps to oxygenate the pond. This is essential if the pond is to be its own ecosystem, supporting wildlife, fish and plants. But, if your fountain spurt is barely more than an ooze, or your waterfall no more than a trickle, then your pump is too small. And conversely, if the water emanating from your drilled urn is more like a burst water main, then the pump is too large.

There are dozens of pump styles, makes and sizes available (see pages 40–41), but the general rule in determining the size of pump required is that it should circulate in one hour a volume of water equivalent to that within the pond system. All pump packs state the circulation volume per hour.

A waterfall makes a strong statement in any garden, and a 'gusher' never fails to impress

WATERFALLS

A waterfall can be made to spill gently over a shallow sill, or gush in torrents over a high ledge, depending on its design and construction. (If the water does not free-fall and is merely tipping and tumbling over rocks, then it is not a waterfall at all, but a 'cascade' – see below.)

A good waterfall is a strong statement: it dominates its setting and can easily overwhelm other features. Unfortunately, it is all too easy to miscalculate water flow, and you can readily end up with a torrent of water crashing from a wide ledge into a tiny pond or, conversely, a tiny trickle into a huge pond. Either will look completely incongruous.

There are prefabricated, moulded units available to act as the 'header' to a waterfall, and these are simple to install. Ensure that they are level from side to side, and that the lip protrudes sufficiently over the pond – and at a suitable height – to enable a body of water to fall into the pond rather than on surrounding ground. The hosepipe linking the pump to the header pool should be carefully hidden.

Sometimes moulded header units are not the right shape or size, in which case it is possible to make the waterfall of concrete and cover it with flat stone or rock, to make it look natural. Some experts recommend using flexible liners over pre-dug ground, to follow the contours of your waterfall feature but, while this is possible, it certainly is not easy. Making a feature out of concrete is likely to be less fraught, and longer lasting.

If making your own header pool from concrete, use any of the same mix recipes (see pages 19–20) as for the concrete pool, and make sure that the header pool itself is some 15cm (6in) deep. This isn't deep enough to support fish or plant life, but is deep enough for water to remain within the depression, even during hot weather.

A more natural effect can be created by adding the edging and base stone while the concrete is still damp. Crucially, the edges must be raised and level in the horizontal plane so that water is distributed evenly throughout the basin.

The grotto waterfall

This is one further distinctive type, where water emits from a fairly high header basin, and falls directly in front of some sort of cavern. This

Garden caves or grottoes make a spectacular feature, and may be home to shade-loving ferns

25

Two cascade styles: ABOVE: Gentle flowing of water from a hidden source into a pool. BELOW: A pond is the source for this cascade, which flows into a stream

cavern can be easily created with concrete and, once established, can be a haven for amphibious wildlife, as well as natural ferns and lichens. Alternatively, by installing the pump and outlet within the recesses of the cavern, and by raising the level of the cavern, you can give the illusion that the water is coming out of the cavern and falling into the pond.

CASCADES

The archetypal definition of a cascade is a small stream, purposefully tumbling over rocks, boulders and pebbles on its downward journey to a pool at the bottom of a slope. With the cascade itself comes the delicate

sound of water splashing, trickling and gurgling, so creating an aura of tranquility.

Most garden cascades are modelled to appear natural, but modern and contemporary equivalents, using sheets of glass, stainless steel and wooden channels, are becoming more popular.

Prefabricated sections, available from most large garden centres in kit form, can be made from thin, lightweight concrete (fairly natural-looking), whilst others are made from shiny fibreglass or plastic. Whilst these latter sections are convenient to install, it is an almost impossible task to make them appear 'natural'. These artificial cascade units can be bought as a short, self-contained header pool/cascade, or as several units which fit together to make longer courses. Even though

This style of cascade could also be referred to as a 'water staircase'

A 'standard' fountain – but there are many styles of water jet to choose from

these come, more or less, as ready-made cascades, you will certainly have to spend some time on preparation work if the whole thing is to look authentic.

A domestic garden cascade can be fairly vertical, with a series of rocks protruding from each other forming the water course, to a shallow nearly level course, where the water appears more as a stream.

In practically every way, a cascade should be treated as if it were a waterfall, even though there is no significant free-falling of water.

A water staircase

French and Italian designers in centuries past made great use of the 'water staircase', by using lengths of concrete drainage pipe, or some such, set in a bed of concrete. Each succeeding length of pipe is set below and slightly out from its predecessor thus forming a staircase with rounded steps, down which sparkling, silvery water will tumble. Disguise the ends of the pipes with rocks or plants. This type of feature works best if there is sufficient water flowing over it, so do not skimp on the size of pump.

Facts & Figures 12

To calculate the volume of water in your pond, measure the length, width and depth of the pond in feet and multiply these together. Multiply the result by 6.25 to give the volume in gallons.

FOUNTAINS

Until fairly recently, most garden fountains were simple patterned sprays of water emerging from a pool. Now there are many options, ranging from sophisticated, grand affairs to small-scale child-safe features.

On the following pages I have made a selection of modern alternatives, together with some simple rules which must be followed if the chosen fountain is to be successful.

Wall-mounted lion's head

This is usually cast into a block, made from concrete or reconstituted stone. A small pipe feeds water through the back and into the mouth, so this needs to be built into a backing wall from the outset. Water pours either directly into a pool below, or into a small suspended reservoir, which can then either overflow into a larger pool below, or be recirculated. Be aware that the smaller the reservoir, the greater the danger of it running dry, through evaporation, in hot weather.

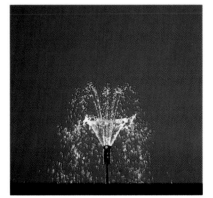

Two-tier fountain

Three-tier fountain

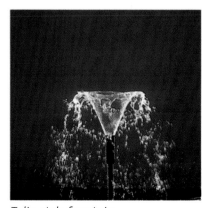

Bell, or sheet fountain

Variable calyx-style fountain

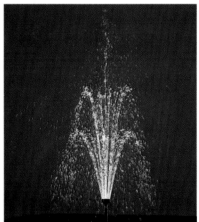

Geyser fountain

Tulip-style fountain

ABOVE: Geyser-style fountains provide a loud splash, and move a high volume of water

RIGHT: Small fountains splashing and bubbling onto a pebble base are easy to install

Geyser 'foam' jets

These are designed to suck in air and mix it with the water to produce a lively column of foaming water which, with an appropriate pump and nozzle, can reach a height of a metre (3ft) or more.

'Bell' jets

These compress a flow of water from a nozzle, deflecting it outwards and downwards to produce a glassy 'mushroom' of water. Lighting can produce dramatic results with this type of fountain, but you must make sure that the pond water is not dirty or full of debris.

Solar-powered fountains

These are now becoming widely available, and more efficient. Their output is not always as good or as substantial as conventional fountains and pumps, but this technology does make it possible to have a modest fountain in a place to where it is difficult to run electricity.

LEFT: A bell fountain requires clean water

Bubbling stones, millstones and 'boulder' fountains

In most cases these are suspended by means of a strong steel grid – sometimes with pebbles and/or rocks – over an underground tank of water. Kits are available from most large garden centres. They include a small plastic reservoir and a plastic cover with a central hole for a fountain on a submersible pump below. Check the water level in the reservoir in hot weather.

Installing a pebble fountain: **1.** *Make a hole in which to fit the reservoir.* **2.** *Line the hole with sand and place the reservoir into position, making sure it is level.* **3.** *Place the pump housing and nozzle and fill with water.* **4.** *Arrange washed pebbles over the pump housing platform.* **5.** *Surround the area with plants and paving – and switch on!*

Installing an egg-style fountain

If you would prefer to see a piece of modern 'art' – something that would be both a focal point and a talking point – this smooth, high density concrete egg fountain has a timeless, contemporary feel. Dimensions of the egg stone are: height 50cm (19³/₄in); width 38cm (15in), and weight 80kg (176lb).

1. *Excavations are started for housing the fountain 'liner' or 'reservoir'. A layer of builders' sand is required in the base of the hole to protect the liner from sharp stones*

2. *The liner is placed in to the hole to check for depth and level – a spirit level is crucial*

3. *More sand is required to protect the sides and lips of the liner, and all edge levels should be checked. The liner is finally put into position, level checked and then more sand used to in-fill and pack the sides*

4. *Rubber tubing, which is cut to fit, needs to be threaded through the egg fountain and then connected to the pump*

5. *The egg is placed into position, and a final check for levels is made*

6. *Pebbles are placed over the inspection cover to complete the effect, and new plants surround the whole structure*

7. *Within just a few weeks, the area looks established*

CONTAINERS

Water barrels, pots, urns, tubs, baths, vases, and so on, whether self-contained units or linked to a larger pond, really add a different dimension to the garden. Any container that can hold water is a potential above-ground pond but it should, of course, be ornamental and decorative.

These containers can be placed almost anywhere in the garden but, because they are small in comparison with a whole pond, it makes sense to site them near a sitting area, or where people will spend an amount of time: on a patio, path, or close to house windows would be suitable sites. Placed to brighten up a dull corner, they can make perfect alternatives to pots of annuals and conifers.

The most important factor is that of light, particularly if you're anticipating growing flowering water plants such as waterlilies. Do not site the container in a dark corner, but nor should it be in full sun for the hottest part of the year, otherwise evaporation will become a problem.

Another factor is that of running power out to the container, for you will almost certainly need a pump to move the water.

Many of the metal, plastic or ceramic containers in the above-mentioned styles will be watertight, but water barrels – or more correctly half-barrels – could well be authentic old-style barrels made by coopers, where open air exists between the wood slats. In this case, we need to make judicious use of the familiar PVC liner.

For relatively little outlay, a container water feature can become an attraction, a talking point and, almost, part of the family.

Preparing a water barrel:

1. Line the container with butyl or rubber sheeting

2 & 3. Staple it in position

4. With sharp scissors trim away the surplus

5. Fill the barrel with water

6. Introduce small aquatic plants

7. In a week or two the barrel will appear established

STREAMS

Most of us want our water features to look 'natural', but ponds often need to go against walls, or next to (or indeed on) patios: hardly 'natural' settings. But a garden stream can look really natural. Even though it is merely a stretch of water going from one place to another, this is exactly the sort of phenomenon that is found in the wild.

In all cases, of course, a man-made stream will contain water that is circulated by a pump. Pumps obviously vary hugely in their performance, and it is crucial that you choose one that will provide the desired effect. For example, a small pump in a very wide or deep stream would produce an imperceptible and completely ineffective flow.

Facts & Figures 13

When choosing the hosepipe to circulate water from your pump, it is important to choose one with the correct diameter, otherwise the water flow can be restricted. The recommended diameters for maximum flow are:

13mm =	1,150 lph (litres per hour)	253 gph (gallons per hour)
19mm =	2,300 lph	506 gph
25mm =	3,600 lph	792 gph
32mm =	6,800 lph	1495 gph
38mm =	13,600 lph	2991 gph

RIGHT: A useful design tip is to bend the line of stepping stones

Garden streams can be made to look entirely natural

The stream should be made dead level, so that it remains full once the pump is switched off. And, when the pump is off, your 'stream' will become a shallow, elongated pond.

One of the trickiest decisions when creating a stream is how to make it suddenly 'appear' in the garden, and then 'disappear' further along. A gurgling stream usually ends up emanating from large pipes or from beneath a stone slab; it will almost certainly disappear in the same way. Most of the gullies the water will travel along are made from concrete, stone or brick, and are either straight or gently curving. Flexible liner can be used, but use gravel, sand, stones, bricks or boulders to give the water a rippling texture and help conceal the shiny PVC or plastic.

If an abrupt change of direction is required some way along the stream, it is best to cover the stream at that point with some sort of chamber, so that water can enter it from one direction and leave in another. Such a chamber could also be used to hide the beginning or end of the stream.

STEPPING STONES

As most (human) visitors to a pond will stand on the edge and look towards the other side, across the surface of the water, one can miss

beauty and activity practically at one's feet. Stepping stones can change all that: from here one can look back towards the pond edge.

Whilst stepping stones are generally meant for access across the pond, and so are designed to be in more or less a straight line, a useful design trick is to cluster a few of them to provide a better viewing (and maintenance) platform.

If the size of your pond allows, go for large stones that you can stand on with both feet or, even better, that you can crouch or kneel on. This will enable you to enjoy the pond at close quarters for a longer time.

Supporting the stones within the pond is not always easy, but the stones must always end up perfectly stable and level, with no chance of them toppling over. This means that each must have a plinth or column virtually the same size as the stepping stone, allowing for only a minimal overhang. Each column has to be built up from

This gravel 'beach' will enable pond creatures to enter and exit the water safely

the floor of the pond and end at a point where the stepping stone appears to float on the surface of the water.

Building onto the floor of a concrete pond is easy. A vertical column of bricks, blocks or stone can be simply built up – using mortar – to the required height.

Ponds made from flexible liners are a little more tricky. It is not ideal to place mortar directly onto the single layer of the base liner as pool liners may be damaged if the ground underneath has not been suitably prepared, so a further protective film – perhaps thick PVC – should be placed on top of the liner before the column is built up on a thick bed of soft sand mortar.

Pre-moulded pools may have been installed with air gaps underneath – sometimes this is unavoidable. If a heavy weight, such as a stepping stone pillar, is applied directly over these, the plastic could buckle and split. It can, therefore, be risky placing columns in these pools.

Pieces of natural stone fit well into natural or informal ponds, and are available in all sorts of shapes and sizes, but they may eventually become rather slippery and, therefore, hazardous. There are obviously plenty of manufactured slabs to choose from – square, round, rectangular, hexagonal – but they are all of a limited size.

Timber decking squares can be used, but not if they have been treated with any toxic substances, which might wash off into the water. Hardwoods, cedar or any other naturally resilient timbers, are better than pressure-treated softwoods.

'BEACHES'

A sandy, muddy or stony 'beach', along one edge of a largish pond, can be eye-catching – it will set the scene for a completely different range of plants, and be a wonderful attraction for wildlife. Boulders, pebbles and even shells can be introduced to give the effect of the foreshore. If you desire it, an adjacent part of the garden could be given over to shingle, where an upturned boat could be at permanent rest, and deck chairs placed for looking at and sitting on – even the garden shed could be converted to look like a beach hut!

It is quite possible that the beach will occupy at least as much space as the pond itself. If a liner is

A sand area for children can be separated from the water by decorative decking

used, it will mean extending it a metre (3ft) or more in one particular direction – don't be tempted to create the beach all the way around the pond: this would take up a huge amount of space and look ugly.

Excavation of the beach area should begin at its farthest point from the pond, with a vertical cut going down to about 25cm (9in). It can then slope very slightly down towards the main area of the pool before finally going down at about 45° into the deepest part of the pond. The laying of the liner is as for laying an ordinary pond (see page 17).

The only negative thing about a home-made freshwater 'beach', is that algae might grow in the shallow water – something which rarely happens in constantly washed seawater pools. However, most algae can be controlled by using an algacide from time to time.

Muddy beaches

For one of these you will first need to build a fairly solid 15cm (6in) high retaining wall of old turves. Site this about 20cm (8in) back from the beginning of the 45° slope. To help keep the wall of turves in position, the bottom turf should be much longer – perhaps a metre (3ft) – and draped over the edge, down into the deeper part of the pond. You then need to fill the area between the vertical part of the liner at the far end and the turf wall with a heavy clay loam (available as loam compost and sold in bags). Once the soil is in place, compact it and rake it so that the far end is at the same level as the adjacent garden soil or lawn. Next, slope the compacted soil gradually downwards until it meets the top of the turf wall; then, when the pond is filled, the water level will rise above the turf wall and be absorbed into the compacted soil to form the mud beach.

RIGHT: Japanese-style bamboo features, like this shishi-odoshi, are becoming very popular

Sandy beaches

Similar to the mud beach, but this one can expand beyond the vertical section of liner. The sand within it will be wet, becoming progressively dry towards the furthest distance from the pond, whilst the sand outside of the liner will be as damp as the surrounding soil, or bone dry on a hot summer's day. Instead of a turf wall, the retaining wall for a sandy beach should be made from stone, mortared to hold it in place.

The types of planting used are important. Ornamental grasses, with spiky phormiums, yuccas and cordylines forming the backdrop, would be wholly appropriate.

JAPANESE-THEMED WATER FEATURES

Another option is a water garden with a wider theme – something in the style of a country, such as Japan, is the most popular.

A Japanese influence can bring an exotic and often sub-tropical feel to the garden, although the preconceived image of a Japanese garden rarely equates with that of the traditional art form. With such diverse cultures it is difficult to appreciate all aspects of each other's artistic creations, and a garden which adheres in every way to the influence of the Orient is unlikely to satisfy all the requirements of a modern western family.

However, the Japanese 'feel' can be achieved by planting, by the use of oriental materials like bamboo, by recreating some of the fundamental principles of Japanese landscape design and, of course, by appropriate use of water. In any Japanese-style garden water is central to the scheme, whether it be in the form of an elegantly shaped extensive pool, or as a simple bamboo shishi-odoshi (deer scarer), periodically spilling water into a bowl.

The shape of a 'Japanese' pool does not matter too much – as long as it is neither perfectly square nor round – for Japanese gardening is about creating a picture that brings the landscape of the countryside into the garden in a much reduced form. Islands can figure prominently, or mountainous representations, which are generally large rocks generously planted or closely associated with shrubby evergreens like the Japanese azalea or maple.

The oriental garden also uses the shoreline creatively. Rocks and planting create niches and promontories and, where water enters a pool from a stream, planting must conceal the entry.

A low, flat island alludes to a moor, and is

usually planted with grasses, sedges and irises, while tidal islands are represented by almost completely submerged rocks interspersed with a tiny grassy planting.

Running water also figures strongly, and it is not confined to wandering streams, rills and cascades – it is even found in bamboo pipework. Large stones and coloured gravels that

complement and contrast with each other are also used just beneath water level along the pool edge.

Of the greatest importance, however, is the choice and arrangement of plants: not all need be from the Orient, but they must look right. Choose bamboos, grasses, irises, primulas and ferns. Where water is the focal point it is fun, and wholly appropriate, to grow a lotus.

The second type of pump is designed to be used out of the water; this is the surface-only pump that is intended for use on dry land. This has the advantage of being extremely powerful, so water can be pumped over large distances, or very high for a spectacular fountain display. It should be housed in a dry, well-ventilated area like a garage or shed, so as to avoid the problems associated with mixing electricity with water (although there are in fact diesel- and petrol-powered versions). Because surface-only pumps are not under water, they can be stripped down and repaired more readily. These pumps are, however, expensive. Neither do they come with many of the 'extras', such as connectors, strainers, hoses, and so on, which will be necessary components to the finished system, and all add to the cost.

The third and final type is the dual-purpose pump system, that can be used as a submersible pump or a surface pump. Some makes need to be housed at a lower level than the water level, so a separate tank is required. However, these pumps offer the flexibility for you to change your mind about their siting and use.

Of course, if you want to operate features like a waterfall and fountain independently, fitting one pump for each feature might prove more satisfactory.

The performance of any pump is affected by the following variables: water temperature, pipe width and length, any angles in the pipework or connectors and the number of water features connected to the pump. With specific features there are such factors as the intended heights of fountains and falls, and the volume of water. All of these can bring about friction loss which will affect your vertical head, that is, the maximum height to which the pump can deliver water. For all of these reasons, it is generally advisable to buy a pump that slightly exceeds the maximum amount of flow that your feature(s) will need. To calculate the right size of pump for your pond, you first need to ascertain the volume of water (see Facts & Figures Tip 12, page 29). You will need a pump that can circulate a

A typical modern submersible pump will enable the pond-keeper to run a fountain or waterfall

Old-fashioned water pump features will need to make use of a modern electric pump to work properly

ACCOUTREMENTS

Pumps

Let's face it, if you want something other than a still pond, then you are going to have to invest in a pump – unless you are lucky enough to have a natural stream or waterfall in your garden. There are essentially three types of water pump (other than the combined pump and filter sets which we will come to in the next chapter). The first, and most common, is the submersible pump, which sits within the body of water in the pond; this is attached to a hosepipe, which carries the circulated water up and away.

volume equivalent to the total volume in your pond every two hours. All good pumps will declare on the packaging the quantity of water they will move, so this is not a difficult decision. What is difficult, however, is choosing from the dozens of makes and models available.

Lighting

This can work its magic and bring water alive at night, particularly during warm, summer evenings. Interesting effects can be created by using coloured lights to illuminate water descending down a waterfall or cascade, or on the upward and downward flow of a fountain. Witness some of our grand public fountains in city centres: they make spectacular night-time displays.

This may sound like something only a technical expert would attempt. Not so. Modestly priced kits can be bought from most garden centres, and with them often come different coloured lights. Sophisticated versions even change colours with moving discs travelling across the bulbs.

Pond lights can be completely submerged. They are available in a range of styles, some with coloured lenses

Lighting will transform a pond or patio area at night

The installation of lighting requires a degree of care and attention, as with all electrical appliances outdoors. Low-voltage lighting is particularly easy and quick to install, with simple push-fit connections. You can even combine in-pond lights with garden lighting on the same cable.

For a circular pool, measure from the centre to the side and square it: multiply the result by 3.14. Multiply this by the depth of the pool (in feet) and multiply the result by 6.25 for the volume in gallons. Take a minute to digest this and try to work it out for yourself – you really don't need to be Einstein!

If you desire to know the volume of your pond in litres it is easiest to convert the total gallonage directly, by referring to a conversion chart. Please note that one gallon equals 4.546 litres.

CHAPTER 4

CLEAN WATER

The most discouraging factor for novice pond-keepers is the murkiness or greenness of the water. It is, therefore, useful to have an appreciation of the science of water, even if you don't understand it completely.

Essentially, 'green' water is the effect produced by millions of microscopic plants – actually algal cells – in suspension. This type of algae is invariably caused by an imbalance of pond water nutrients, and the culprits are usually fish. These produce both ammonia and phosphate as waste which, as every keen gardener knows, make excellent fertilizers. Introducing aquatic plants and oxygenators into the water while it is green would be a waste, because algae prevent light from reaching the plants, so their growth is restricted.

So, if you are going to invest in a pond, it will pay to have a reasonably clear understanding of the life cycle of the water before you begin.

LIFE CYCLE OF A POND

CLEAN WATER
(either as fresh mains water when the pond is filled, or as on-going 'clear' water)

USED WATER
(caused by soil, run-off from surrounding ground, fish waste and excess, i.e. uneaten, fish food)

DISEASED WATER
(if water is not treated heterotrophic bacteria, which carry diseases, settle in the water)

RAIN & WATER
(rain from the atmosphere fills our ponds and tops up our mains supplies)

EXCESS
(nitrates and phosphates not able to be absorbed by plants will lead to problems – methane gas, blanketweed, algae, acid water, lack of oxygen at night, etc)

AMMONIA
(this will be created in severe instances)

OXYGEN & NITROGEN
(water plants repay us by returning these two elements to the atmosphere)

PLANT FOODS
(nitrates – not nitrites – and phosphates are all good to have, in small quantities, in all ponds, for consumption by aquatic plants)

NITRIFYING BACTERIA
(nitrites are broken down by nitrifying bacteria)

NITRITE
(and if the water is not treated once ammonia is created, nitrite will be formed. This is particularly deadly to fish)

Green water is caused by millions of microscopic plants – algae

It starts off clean, then gets polluted with fish waste and soil. These cause ammonia and various other toxicities, which mostly turn into nitrites; these then get broken down in to plant foods (which is good), and the excess causes blanketweed, algae, acidic water and oxygen starvation (which is bad).

The accompanying flow-chart will help to put this life cycle into context, but the underlying message is that the water in your pond needs to be healthy.

TESTING AND TREATMENT

As the slightest change to the water chemistry of your pond can have a major effect on the life in it, it is advisable to test the water, and there are a number of kits available that will check levels of pH, ammonia, nitrate, nitrite and protein for you quickly and easily. However, with such a wide choice available, deciding which kit to buy is rather like buying vitamins – do you opt for one to deal with specific needs in mind or try an all-round multi-vitamin for optimum health?

Fortunately there are several kits which include tests for all the following:

Pond water testing kits are available from most garden centres and shops

Facts & Figures 16

Occasionally pond water will turn 'milky'. This is a sure sign that there is a dead fish or other animal decomposing in the vicinity. Get it out as soon as you can, and replace as much water as is reasonable.

pH levels

pH is the measure of acidity or alkalinity of a substance and high levels of them affect the health of your fish and plants. Acidic water is lower than pH6.5, whereas alkaline water is higher than pH7.5. The figure of pH7 and a little either side of it are referred to as being 'neutral'. Most pond fish require a level between pH6.5 and pH7.5. Levels over pH8.5 can restrict plant growth as well as cause stress to your fish, which can lead to infection and disease.

Ammonia

Even the lowest levels of ammonia will stress fish, making them susceptible to infection and disease, so any sign of ammonia should be treated as an emergency situation for fish. High levels of ammonia in pond water are usually caused by over-stocking of fish, or too much detritus (uneaten food, fish waste, decaying plants and even dead insects).

Nitrite and nitrate

If ammonia in the pond is not treated, nitrites and nitrates will form. The former are highly toxic and very dangerous to fish, whilst the latter are non-toxic, and high levels act as plant nutrients, which leads to the growth of algae.

Protein

The build-up of animal proteins in the water is usually due to the remains of food, fish waste and decomposing organisms. If untreated, these will lead to higher pH levels, a build-up of ammonia, nitrites and nitrates.

If the results of your tests have highlighted areas for improvement, then it is essential to take action as soon as possible. For optimum water quality there are various treatments for reducing high levels of pH, ammonia, nitrites and nitrates.

Some general treatments are made from evaporated sea water. These can temporarily block the toxic effects of nitrite in the water and replace electrolytes such as potassium, sodium, chloride, calcium and magnesium, which are all essential for the uptake of oxygen and the release of carbon dioxide and ammonium, which fish lose in times of stress.

There are also treatments that can be used for aesthetic problems such as unsightly sludge, algae or surface foam. In most cases these will come in the form of sachets of dry granules which are sprinkled over the pond. Be careful not to exceed the dosage.

The chemical treatments for clearing cloudy water – generally caused by suspended algae – work by bonding some of the suspended particles. This makes them heavy enough to either fall to the bottom of the pond, or to be removed by filtration (see below).

Finally, if you need to place your fish in fresh tap-water, there are treatments to neutralize the water and make it safe for them. Tap-water is usually treated by local authorities to ensure that it is fit for human consumption. However, this means that chemicals such as chlorine and chloramine are added, and these are harmful to fish. A tap-water conditioner eliminates these chemicals, and neutralizes harmful metal ions, making the water suitable for your pond.

POND FILTRATION AND UV CLARIFIERS

Why bother with a filtration system in your pond? After all, natural ponds and larger still waters don't have artificial filters, and they can generally support fish quite happily. Well, it's not quite as simple as that: a good filter is the only way to keep water crystal clear, while at the same time keep fish in tip-top condition.

The wild fish in our rivers and lakes don't always get it their own way, of course. They are at the behest of the elements, natural predators and, of course, the angler himself. However, in one important respect, they have a major advantage over their domesticated pond-dwelling cousins – they can swim off to pastures new if the water quality around them deteriorates.

Facts & Figures 17

It is pure folly to consider keeping koi in a pond without a filter. The waste from one of these fish over 35cm (14in) in length dramatically increases. A number of them in a pond would put a huge demand on any filtration system, so with no system at all the chance of keeping even small specimens is extremely slim and a waste of money considering how much they cost.

Garden ponds are quite limited environments when contrasted with the natural vastness of rivers and lakes, and pond fish are completely at our mercy.

Before we go any further, we must clarify something: clear water is not necessarily clean water. Having the bottom of a 1m (3ft) pond in clear, visible focus is very much a priority for us but fish don't generally care what they can or cannot see. For example, sight plays a tiny part in the life of our wild carp, which spend virtually all their life stirring up sediment into an impenetrable cloud in their search for small invertebrate food!

A large planted pond with few fish is indeed viable without a filter, but the 'safe' stocking rate for fish is 50–76cm (20–30in) length of fish per 4546 litres (1000 gal). At this rate you would be lucky to spot the fish between the plants, unless it was feeding time, or they were basking in the sun. A fountain, which increases the oxygen level

Facts & Figures 18

With UV lamp wattages, a safe ratio is ten watts per 4546 litres (1000 gal) – manufacturers' claims vary widely. But, if your pond is very shallow, contains few plants with surface-shading leaves, or is exposed to full sunlight for most of the day, then it's a good idea to go for a lamp that is up a size from that recommended for your pond volume.

This pressurized filter is typical of the modern generation of filters for hiding near ponds

in the water, would mean that the pond was capable of supporting a greater head of fish, but in nothing like the numbers made possible by even the simplest filtration package.

Filters, therefore, have a number of worthy applications: they allow us to have more, healthier fish; they help to clear the water and, more importantly, are essential in cleaning a pond. Specifically, filtration removes debris, while at the same time the inhospitable nitrogenous detritus caused by fish waste, the toxins caused by rotting plant material and general detritus are converted into less harmful substances.

How filters work

There are three basic methods of filtration: chemical, mechanical and biological. Each has a part to play, in varying degrees of importance:

Chemical filtration

Here, the filter medium exerts a chemical influence on the water as it passes through. We can generally discount this as a long-term filtration option, although there are times when it is useful. For example, zeolite is a chemical filter medium and is capable of absorbing ammonia from the water. It comes in the form of light grey or light brown chippings, made from hydrated silicates of calcium and aluminium, sometimes with sodium and potassium.

Chemical filtration really comes into its own when a pond and filter are first set up, and the chemical and nitrogenous balance in the water has not been stabilized; in other words, the system is going through the process of maturation.

Mechanical filtration

This is the mechanical removal of solid waste as the water passes through a suitable medium, such as foam, synthetic fibre or even gravel. The trapped solids are periodically removed from the system by hand. The filter can then be flushed through with clean water, under a tap.

Many modern mechanical filters have an in-built Ultra Violet (UV) clarifier, and they work together to give clear water. A UV clarifier is not a filter in itself, but it makes algae clump together and they then strain out easily as the water they are floating in passes through the filter. Removal of solids also means that the most important aspect of filtration – the biological stage – works efficiently.

Biological filtration

This method makes use of natural biological processes to purify the water. It is also, arguably, the most important element in keeping fish alive. Although they vary in design, all biological filters support a colony of aerobic bacteria (i.e. those that flourish in oxygen-rich conditions) which convert toxic ammonia into progressively less harmful substances that are then recycled. This is the so-called 'nitrogen cycle'.

A quick run-through of the biological filtration process is thus:

1. *During decomposition, fish waste and other organic debris is converted to ammonia compounds by bacteria and fungi in the pond. These compounds can be injurious to the fish.*
2. *A biological filter will begin its work by trapping larger dirt particles in the first layer of foam (this is purely 'mechanical').*

3. *Nitrosomonas bacteria, contained within the biological filter, then consume the harmful ammonia compounds and convert them to nitrites.*

4. *Unfortunately, the nitrites are just as toxic to the fish as the ammonia. Again, the filter comes into play with a population of Nitrobacter bacteria that convert the nitrites to nitrates. The nitrates do not affect the fish but fertilize the pond plants and algae.*

5. *The cycle is completed, because the pond fish eat the plants and algae.*

Filter designs

There is a wide choice of filters available, catering for everyone, from the beginner with a small pond, to the specialist with a large pool full of valuable fish.

The main problem with smaller pump-fed filters is that they are not adequately equipped to deal with the solids loading – they fall down mechanically, requiring such frequent maintenance that pond-keeping ceases to be a pleasure. If you can afford it, and have room for it, opt for a filter that is larger than the minimum recommended for your size of pond. The larger the filter, the longer the intervals will be between cleanings.

A major drawback with the larger filters, however, is that they are usually highly visible. Downflow models have to be installed fully above the ground, and upflow versions can be only partially buried. If they are installed at the top of a waterfall it is quite easy to conceal them, but then the greater 'head' (the distance between pond surface and filter outflow point) will reduce pumping capacity.

A pump-fed, pressurized filter with integral UV clarifier is the answer. This can be sited anywhere around the pond – topping a cascade, buried in the adjoining ground to lid level or simply stood on a level base. Because water exits under pressure it can be piped up to a waterfall header pool, or simply returned via a hose to the pond.

Pressurized filters actually force dirty water through the foam media rather than relying on gravity, and so many more solids can be trapped before the foam needs a clean. Before this happens, signalled by a drop in exit flow rate, the foam will become a progressively more efficient mechanical filter. The UV lamp is contained within the pressurized canister and all water has to pass by it on its way back to the pond.

Filter pumps

The pump that drives a filter must be of the solids-handling type, quite different from the one used to power a fountain. Fountain pumps do incorporate a strainer, but this is partly so their impellers are not clogged and partly to prevent dirt particles travelling up to the fountain nozzle and blocking the jet.

Solids-handling pumps are designed to take all the debris out of the pond and into the filter. Their impellers, depending on the model, will handle solids from 8–10mm ($\frac{5}{16}$–$\frac{6}{16}$in) in diameter, which means that the poor gardener is not constantly hauling up the pump to unblock it.

OXYGENATING PLANTS

Most books about water gardening include the bit about pond 'weed' in the section about pond plants, along with the rather more decorative flowering plants. In reality, however, there is only one real reason to have pondweeds, or oxygenating plants, in your pond, and that is to provide oxygen, which in turn helps to keep the water stable and in good condition. Of all the plants we can add to our ponds, these are perhaps the least interesting, yet they are almost certainly the most important. Let's start with the basics.

If there are too many fish, or not enough plants (particularly the oxygenating type) in your pond, the water becomes short of dissolved oxygen. This manifests itself in fish either gasping for air at the surface, or lurking at the bottom, utterly disinterested in their food. If you add outside influences such as lack of water movement, and a spell of still, sultry weather that warms up the water so it can hold even less dissolved oxygen, you can very readily end up with some extremely sick fish.

Increasing the oxygen level in the water is not difficult. You can turn on the fountain or waterfall (if you have one), which will add and mix oxygen into the water as it tumbles and turns. However, if you have a still pond, the simplest thing to do is to make sure you have a plentiful and permanent supply of cheap and easy-to-grow oxygenating plants.

These are usually green, they rarely flower and seem to spend their lives suspended in the water, growing rapidly when your back is turned and never when you want them to. By day they convert dissolved carbon dioxide, given off by the fish, into oxygen. They also consume minerals and nutrients that otherwise would be used by opportunist and troublesome algae. A good selection of oxygenating plants will also provide effective cover for all manner of water creatures; fish will be afforded some protection against marauding herons, and spawning grounds will be provided for fish, amphibious and insectivorous wildlife.

Most garden centres will offer oxygenating plants from outside tanks and they are usually sold as small bunches of stems linked by a heavy metal weight. You just have to drop these bunches into the pond – you don't need planting baskets or compost. The weights will take the bases of the bunches down, and they will find their own level, depending on the amount of leaves, and start to grow.

Most oxygenators will grow rapidly, especially during warm summers, and can cause the pond to become congested. You should, therefore, hook out a few bucketsful of excess weed, perhaps two or three times during the summer period. This will, curiously, make the weed grow faster, and in turn make it more efficient at filtering and conditioning the water. Carefully check through the foliage as you're removing it, spread it out by the side of the pond and leave it for a day so that any creatures caught up in it, and which can crawl back into the water, are given the best chance.

Add the semi-dried weed to the compost heap. On no account be inclined to take it to your local

Canadian pondweed is an excellent oxygenator, but needs to be controlled

pond or stream to keep it alive. Many misguided aquarists and pond owners have done this in the past, thus introducing plants that have quickly crowded out our native pond plant species and upsetting the whole ecology of our natural waterways.

It's a good idea to select several species of oxygenator so that a variety of wildlife will be attracted. All wild pond-inhabiting creatures have their particular likes and dislikes, and a variety of foliage shapes and growth habits will offer the most habitats. Some of the best oxygenators include:

Autumn starwort (*Callitriche hermaphroditica*)
A delicate plant, with vivid green foliage and fragile stems, that grows all year. It is prone to damage by heavy-finned fish.

Canadian pondweed (*Elodea canadensis*)
Probably the most commonly seen oxygenator, it is hardy, vigorous and ideal for new ponds.

Curled pondweed (*Potamogeton crispus*)
The long, crinkled leaves can be slow to establish, but are very sturdy, making the plant particularly good for ponds with waterfalls or fountains.

Hornwort (*Ceratophyllum demersum*)
This free-floating plant has dark green, feathery foliage, and may need securing by tying to a stone or weight.

Water milfoil (*Myriophyllum aquaticum*)

There are about 40 different water milfoils worldwide, all making superb perennial oxygenating plants with attractive blue-green or brown fern-like leaves in artistic whorls. But there are only a small handful that are regularly found in our domestic outdoor ponds. *Myriophyllum aquaticum* is the most commonly seen, with very dense ferny foliage that emerges stiffly from the water. It is a tropical species and tends to die back in winter to dormant crowns that rest well beneath the surface of the water. These crowns then re-emerge in spring.

Water violet (*Hottonia palustris*)

This floating plant also produces flowers and has immense ornamental value, therefore details about it are included in our next chapter (see pages 56–7).

GENERAL MAINTENANCE

Finally, there are a number of mechanical aids to help us keep our ponds clean and therefore clear:

Nets

Removing floating debris is fairly straightforward – an ordinary pond net will often do the trick, though it needs time and patience if you are chasing small bits of debris around the pond surface.

Pond vacuums

For most of us, the thought of 'cleaning out the pond' fills us with horror because it's a slippery and smelly job. Removing debris and sludge from the bottom of the pond can be fairly difficult, though we are fortunate these days to have aquatic vacuum cleaners to help us out. Remember, however, that a pond vacuum will not turn a cloudy pond into a crystal clear lagoon. It removes the silt, sludge, detritus and potentially toxic substances from the bottom of the pond. Hence algal growth is largely reduced, the water becomes clearer over a period of time, and filter systems are made more efficient. A side benefit is that garden beds and borders will be treated to a fine watery manure which they'll lap up (specially on hungry or chalky soils).

LEFT: Water milfoil (Myriophyllum aquaticum)

Using a pond vacuum will remove silt and sludge from the bottom of the pond

Most pond vacuum sets comprise a collecting tank with motor unit and 10m (over 30ft) of cable, a 5m (16ft) suction hose, a 2.5m (8ft) discharge hose, a hose-end connector, extension tubes and adjustable suction nozzles. Some more sophisticated types even include a radio remote control with battery and holder.

Operating these pond vacuums is not difficult. The unit should always be at least 2m (6ft) away from the pond edge. Place the end of the discharge hose where the muddy water is to be released when the collecting tank is emptied. This effluent can be directed over any bed, ideally between plants to hide any discoloration of the soil. Connect the unit to the power supply via an RCD and switch it on.

Guide the nozzle to the bottom of the pond, and move it slowly and evenly to vacuum up the mud. When the collecting tank has been filled to its maximum level, a float valve automatically switches off the vacuuming operation, indicated by a high-pitched motor noise. At this point, take the nozzle out of the water and tilt the hose up to allow the remaining water to drain into the tank. Then switch off the unit.

Pond scissors

These are supplied with handles around 115cm (45in) long and are very helpful for cutting through dead weeds; they are particularly effective for the dreaded blanketweed, which can smother plants and choke fish.

FURNISHING WITH PLANTS

CHAPTER 5

FLOATING WATER PLANTS

Floating water plants are those that are not anchored by roots, although some do produce a few straggly roots that simply dangle in the water.

These plants tend to die down during late autumn, surviving the winter as dormant 'buds', resting in the mud at the bottom of the pond. In spring, when the weather warms, they burst into life again.

Some floating plants increase their size and number rapidly and, as with the oxygenators discussed in the last chapter, can cause overcrowding in the pond. It is for this reason that there is a restriction in the sale of such plants in some warmer climates, including some of the southern states of the USA, where the winters offer less of a check to their growth.

Let's consider some of the best floating plants:

● Common duckweed (*Lemna minor*)

The origin of the common name is, to say the least, hazy, although ducks on larger ponds and

Duckweed – one doesn't really plant it, it just happens

lakes will certainly nuzzle around looking for small creatures hiding in it. Some fish eat it, and they lurk under the shade it affords. The form that is generally found in garden ponds is *Lemna minor* and, if you introduce it to your pond – either accidentally or on purpose – the pond will soon be covered with a pale lime-green 'carpet'. Don't walk on it though, like a child did when I was visiting Wisley gardens in the 1970s. Fortunately the pond was very shallow, but the youngster had a nasty shock, and so did his parents.

FLOWERS *These appear in summer, and are tiny, grey-white and wholly insignificant.*

LEAVES *Minute almost translucent, deciduous fronds in various shapes, but mostly oval. Thousands of them abut each other to form a dense carpet over the surface of the water. Each individual frond usually produces a single, dangling root.*

CULTIVATION *One doesn't really 'cultivate' duckweed – it just happens! Planting comprises simply dropping several leaves with roots into the pond, generally in spring. It grows best in still, or nearly still water, and in either full sun or light shade. Duckweed is left to its own devices. All you need to do is use a net to thin it out occasionally to prevent it from covering and choking the whole pond.*

HARDINESS *Very hardy, tolerating temperatures as low as -20˚C. Duckweed survives in winter as dormant buds on the bottom of the pond.*

PROPAGATION *Again, one doesn't really 'propagate' duckweed. Just redistribute some of the fronds to a different pond.*

ORIGINS *A one-species plant, originally from the Atlantic side of North America.*

HEIGHT *None – to speak of.*

SPREAD *A couple of individual fronds can increase and cover up to 1m² (9 sq ft) in a year, but thereafter rapid covering of ponds can take place.*

Facts & Figures 21

One of the methods by which common duckweed disperses itself is on the feet of wading birds. Hence you may find that your pond possesses it, when you know with absolute certainty that it has not come in on any new plants.

MINIMUM WATER DEPTH *15cm (6in).*

MINIMUM POND SIZE *Small – up to about 2m² (18 sq ft).*

ALTERNATIVE *Perhaps the best form to choose is the ivy-leaved duckweed (Lemna trisulca). This is less invasive than the common kind and produces a mass of star-shaped leaves, frequently floating just beneath the surface. Lemna gibba, often referred to as the 'thick' or 'gibbous' duckweed, has rounded, swollen leaves and is particularly invasive. Lemna polyrhiza (also known as Spirodela polyrhiza, and commonly referred to as 'great' duckweed) has larger, rounder leaves than the normal kinds, and each has a small 'tuft' of roots attached. Very invasive.*

EXPERT TIP *Most gardening experts are asked how to get rid off duckweed, rather than how to grow it. Be warned: if you don't want it, it is important to check carefully each new water plant for the presence of duckweed before it is introduced to the pond.*

● Fairy moss (*Azolla filiculoides*)

While this is no moss, neither is it a flowering plant. Actually, it is a charming tiny fern that congregates into dense masses. Although it is a native of more temperate climes, it survives quite harsh winters successfully. The simple, short and slender roots absorb nourishment from the pond water. Keeping multiplication under control in a small pond is not a problem but, as plants can eventually cover the whole surface, you should

Azolla fills the available area, then pushes up into ridges to form an impenetrable mat

Facts & Figures 22

As fairy moss (azolla) is a fern growing in water, the derivation of its botanical name shouldn't come as a surprise: from the Greek *azo*, to dry up, and *ollymi*, to kill, i.e. the plant that is killed by drought!

not introduce this into large inaccessible ponds. It will rapidly become out of hand, and a nuisance.

FLOWERS *None.*

LEAVES (OR FRONDS) *Pale blue-green lacy deciduous fronds, only 1cm (½in) across, turning a rich reddish-purple during autumn.*

CULTIVATION *In spring drop a few fronds directly onto the water. Best position is in full sun to light shade. This plant is unreliable in moving water such as caused by a fountain or waterfall. Net out unwanted plants during the growing season. Plants survive winter as submerged dormant buds, but as frost injury is possible some plantlets should be overwintered under glass in a jar of water and soil and kept frost-free.*

HARDINESS *Barely hardy, tolerating temperatures down to -5°C only.*

PROPAGATION *Simply remove a few fronds and introduce them to a new pond during mid-spring.*

ORIGINS *Originally from the warmer parts of North America.*

HEIGHT *Up to 2.5cm (1in).*

SPREAD *Prolific: a single piece is capable of completely covering a small pond within a season.*

MINIMUM POND SIZE *Small to medium – about 3m² (27 sq ft) so that it can be controlled with the use of nets.*

ALTERNATIVE PLANTS *The normal species only is available, and it may sometimes be found under the name* Azolla caroliniana.

EXPERT TIP *Azolla makes a useful addition to tropical aquaria.*

● Frogbit (*Hydrocharis morsus-ranae*)

The flowers of this plant look as if they are trilliums – woodland dwelling plants with only three petals. However, frogbit is a rather beautiful floating aquatic plant. In its native countries it can, if not kept in check, quickly overcrowd and block up small pools and waterways.

FLOWERS *From mid- to late summer, rising above the surface of the water, white three-petalled flowers appear, each with a yellow centre.*

LEAVES *Small, deciduous, rounded or kidney-shaped leaves of green-bronze leaves, both floating and raised above the water surface.*

CULTIVATION *'Planting' consists of simply dropping young plants in the water; this should be done in spring. The best light conditions for frogbit are full sun to very light shade. Thin out established plants several times a year with a net to limit the spread. Water snails have a liking for the leaves, but this is the only problem you are likely to encounter.*

HARDINESS *This plant tolerates temperatures as low as -20°C, and survives the winter as dormant buds.*

PROPAGATION *Carefully remove young plantlets that form on runners (rather like strawberries, but on a much smaller scale). This can be done at any time during the growing season.*

ORIGINS *Northern Europe.*

HEIGHT *Up to 5cm (2in).*

SPREAD *One plant will cover about 1m² (9 sq ft) after a year.*

MINIMUM POND SIZE *Small – to about 3m² (27 sq ft).*

ALTERNATIVE PLANTS *Normally only this species is available.*

EXPERT TIP *Frogbit is always best grown in a still pond, with water that is neutral to alkaline.*

● Water hyacinth (*Eichhornia crassipes*)

This robust free-floating plant is a prolific grower in hot climates. It's an evergreen or semi-evergreen perennial, and flowers during late summer – the more flowers the hotter the summer. Although recommended for the garden pond in summer, it is a plant well suited to indoor water displays and large aquaria.

FLOWERS *Bluish-violet blooms, not unlike small hyacinths, rise above the water surface from mid-summer to early autumn.*

LEAVES *Round, dark and shiny, almost succulent, with strong swollen stems honeycombed inside for buoyancy.*

Facts & Figures 23

Some countries use water hyacinth plants as a form of biological filtration in water treatment works, to effectively treat sewage and remove heavy metals.

The water hyacinth (Eichhornia crassipes) is a worthy pond plant – but is tender

CULTIVATION *Plant water hyacinths in early summer, by placing them into the pond. They perform best in full sun; the more sunlight that beats down upon them, the better they like it. Invasiveness only becomes a problem if the plants are growing in very small ponds. Individual plants can be removed by hand if necessary.*

HARDINESS *It's a tender plant, and will tolerate temperatures only down to 15˚C.*

PROPAGATION *Water hyacinths may be propagated by separating the clumps in spring, or in the autumn as they are removed to their winter quarters.*

ORIGINS *It is so invasive in its natural habitat – tropical South America – that in some parts there are movement orders against it; in the US, federal law forbids shipping it between certain states.*

HEIGHT *Up to 30cm (12in).*

SPREAD *Up to 1m² (9 sq ft) per year.*

MINIMUM POND SIZE *Tiny: even a water barrel or indoor aquarium could sustain a plant or two, but be prepared to thin them out regularly.*

ALTERNATIVE NAME *It is sometimes sold as* Pontaderia crassipes.

EXPERT TIP *Plants are most unlikely to survive a cold winter outdoors, so remove them from the pond during mid-autumn. Divide them, and store them in wet mud or moist pots in a greenhouse or cold frame until the spring. They can be re-sited in the pond from mid-spring onwards, but it is worth hardening them off gradually; the plant tissue will have become tender, and could be damaged if there is a severe late frost.*

Water soldiers (Stratiotes aloides)

● Water soldiers (*Stratiotes aloides*)

This intriguing plant is often described as resembling a floating pineapple top. It's a semi-evergreen perennial, free-floating, and held partly below and partly above the water. Curiously, plants sink and multiply after flowering, and rise again some weeks later, when surplus offsets can be thinned with a net. Stratiotes is a good choice for wildlife ponds.

FLOWERS *Early to late summer. Separate male and female forms, small, creamy white and papery, tucked in the leaf axils. The male flowers are produced in clusters in a pinkish spathe.*

LEAVES *Dark olive green, narrow and stiff-toothed, arranged in neat rosettes.*

CULTIVATION *Water soldiers perform best in full sun. They usually overwinter at the bottom of the pond. Stratiotes can be prolific, but because the individual plants are so large, they can be removed by hand if necessary.*

HARDINESS *Fully hardy (to -15°C).*

PROPAGATION *New plants form as small water buds on spreading stems: they may be propagated by separating the clumps in spring and summer.*

ORIGINS *Found throughout Europe, preferring alkaline or limestone waters (which is why it does not always transfer from one pond to another successfully).*

HEIGHT *Up to 40cm (16in).*
SPREAD *0.4m² (3 sq ft) per year.*
MINIMUM POND SIZE *Small: up to about 2m² (18 sq ft).*
PREFERRED WATER DEPTH *38–90cm (15–36in).*
ALTERNATIVE NAME *Water aloe.*

● Water violet (*Hottonia palustris*)

If you want to grow a floating water plant with attractive flowers held well above the surface of the water, and which doubles as an oxygenator, then you can hardly do better than to choose the water violet. It is a beautiful hardy herbaceous perennial that is not a violet at all, but a member of the primula family – and a fairly rare member at that. The flowers, when combined with leaves that protrude out of the water, give this plant the appearance of a marginal.

FLOWERS *Spikes of white or pale lilac flowers 23cm (9in) high, in early to mid-summer.*

LEAVES *The mid-green feathery leaves which float just below the surface of the water are efficient oxygenators, whilst other less divided leaves are also under the water, but do not oxygenate.*

CULTIVATION *These plants grow best in full sun or medium shade. Individual plants are dropped into the water in spring. In shallow water they will root in the mud at the bottom, but in deeper water will rest just below the surface – at least for the early part of the summer – before throwing up the flower spikes. Thin out excessive growth during the summer. In autumn plants die down and pass the winter as dormant buds, known as turions.*

HARDINESS *Very hardy, tolerating temperatures down to -20°C.*

Facts & Figures 24

As an insurance against losses in the coldest winter weather, keep a few young floating plants in fish tanks (minus the fish), or in jars of soil and water indoors overwinter. They can be planted out from mid-spring onwards, but it is worth hardening them off gradually, as the plant tissue will have become tender, and could be damaged if there is a severe late frost.

The water violet (Hottonia palustris) prefers to grow in still waters

PROPAGATION *In summer. Divide larger plants, or root stem cuttings in wet mud. Gather any submerged seeds in autumn and grow them on in trays of mud.*

ORIGINS *Britain, Northern Europe and Northern Asia.*

HEIGHT *Up to 37cm (15in).*

SPREAD *Will cover up to 1m² (3 sq ft) per year.*

MINIMUM WATER DEPTH *15–45cm (6–18in).*

MINIMUM POND SIZE *Small: up to about 2m² (18 sq ft).*

ALTERNATIVE PLANTS *Hottonia inflata – referred to as the featherfoil – is similar, but is smaller, with white flowers. However, it is rare and difficult to find.*

EXPERT TIP *It prefers still, rather than moving water, so it is best to avoid planting the water violet in ponds fed by cascades or which contain fountains.*

CHAPTER 6

FLOWERING WATER PLANTS

Aquatic plants come into a number of different categories: oxygenating and floating types are two we have already seen. The flowering water plant is another category, and is somewhat larger than the first two. These are plants that grow within the pond, anchored in the mud, or in planting containers, but which have leaves and flowers sitting on top of the water or rising above it.

Waterlilies are the classic flowering water plant but, like other plants in their group, varieties must be chosen very carefully, according to the vigour of their surface spread and the depth of water to which they are most suited.

Branched bur-reed (Sparganium erectum)

FLOWERING AQUATICS

Here are some of the most notable:

● Branched bur-reed (*Sparganium erectum*)

This is a common sight growing wild on the edges of ditches and river banks, but it also makes a super garden plant. It is not technically a reed at all, but has the vague appearance of one. It performs better as a garden plant if sited in deeper water rather than in the shallows or pond margins.

FLOWERS *In summer, small pale green flowers appear, massed in rounded spiky heads or burrs. The female flowers are larger and positioned towards the bases of the branched stalks.*

LEAVES *The leaves are long, green and grass-like; deciduous, or semi-deciduous in milder areas.*

CULTIVATION *During spring plant young specimens directly into the soil in very large pools, or otherwise into planting baskets. The best position is in full sun, but moderate shade is acceptable. Little on-going care is needed, but dead stems and leaves should be removed in autumn.*

HARDINESS *Very hardy, tolerating temperatures as low as -20˚C.*

PROPAGATION *Divide the plants in spring, or sow fresh seeds into mud in submerged pots.*

ORIGINS *Evidence exists that this plant is native to Europe from the Arctic Circle downwards, through North Africa, Asia, the western Himalayas, Japan, North America and even south-east Australia.*

HEIGHT *Up to 1.5m (5ft) after three years, depending on the depth of water.*

SPREAD *Up to 60cm (2ft).*

PREFERRED WATER DEPTH *30cm (12in).*

Golden club (Orontium aquaticum) *needs to be grown in an open, sunny place for best effect*

RECOMMENDED POND SIZE *Medium to large.*
ALTERNATIVE PLANTS *Normally this is the only sparganium to be seen, but it may sometimes be sold under its alternative but less correct name S. ramosum.*
EXPERT TIP *Try to avoid planting the burr reed in shallow water where it will soon become a menace.*

● Golden club (*Orontium aquaticum*)

This slow-growing hardy perennial deserves a position in full view so that visitors can fully appreciate the wonderful golden flower spikes. It's an accommodating plant, and can be grown centrally in a small pool – where it can be truly spectacular – or near the edge of larger ponds.
FLOWERS *Orontium is a member of the arum family, but differs in that it does not produce a leafy 'spathe'; in this plant the spathe is reduced to a* small, insignificant structure at the base of the long white spikes. These spikes – which appear mid-spring to early summer – each have golden tips like lit candles, and are held just above water level. Small green fruits develop under the surface of the water when the spikes fade.
LEAVES *The lance-shaped leaves are deciduous and almost succulent in appearance. They are dark*

Facts & Figures 25

The Latin name for golden club – orontium – derives from the Greek, and it is believed to have originated from the fact that these plants were first seen growing in the Syrian river Orontes.

Mare's tail (Hippuris vulgaris) has short, narrow leaves spiralling up and along short stems

purplish-green beneath and silvery on top. In shallow water the leaves form an erect clump, but can be floating or partly submerged elsewhere.

CULTIVATION *Plant young plants in spring, or dormant rhizomes in winter. In ponds use aquatic baskets; ordinary (but deep) garden soil is suitable if orontium is to be grown as a marginal plant. A position in full sun or very light shade is best. Plants are generally trouble-free. Keep more invasive plants away from orontium. In autumn, remove dead foliage, and apply a mulch of leaf-mould to land-* grown plants. Take care not to disturb the plants once they are established.

HARDINESS *Fairly hardy, tolerating winter temperatures as low as -15°C.*

PROPAGATION *Sow ripe seeds in summer, in moist soil or under glass. Rhizomes can be divided in spring, each segment with a node. Cuttings taken from the roots, in spring, can also be successful.*

ORIGINS *A one-species plant, originally from the Atlantic side of North America.*

HEIGHT *Up to 30cm (12in) above water.*

SPREAD *Up to 60cm (2ft).*

PREFERRED WATER DEPTH *10–45cm (4–18in).*

RECOMMENDED POND SIZE *Small – up to about 2m² (18 sq ft).*

ALTERNATIVE PLANTS *The normal species only is available.*

EXPERT TIP *Orontiums seldom require dividing. They should only be disturbed if they are being propagated, or if the baskets in which some may be growing, have become crowded.*

Facts & Figures 26

The dried seeds of golden club used to be eaten by the native American Indians, and it is said that cattle would regularly feed on the foliage.

● Mare's tail (*Hippuris vulgaris*)

As a gardening magazine editor of two decades standing, I have been asked more times than I care to remember, how to eradicate one of the worst weeds known to humankind – horsetail *(Equisetum vulgare)*. The plant we are recommending here bares no relation to that weed, although the name sounds similar (and to add to the confusion there is at least one good equisetum that is sometimes grown as a marginal plant)! *Hippuris vulgaris* is an attractive perennial, and in calm waters in many parts of the world its strongly spreading rhizome forms large colonies. It will not escape notice, even in a small pond.

FLOWERS *Minute, insignificant green flowers appear during summer.*

LEAVES *The strength of the plants comes with its foliage. In spirals up the stalks, come many short, narrow, deciduous needle-like leaves.*

CULTIVATION *Set young plants or rhizomes into planting baskets during spring. A site in full sun, or lightly shaded, is preferred. Remove dead foliage in the autumn.*

HARDINESS *Very hardy, tolerating temperatures as low as -20˚C.*

PROPAGATION *Divide the plants in spring.*

ORIGINS *Throughout Europe.*

HEIGHT *Up to 30cm (12in) depending on the depth of water in which they are growing.*

SPREAD *Up to 45cm (18in) after three years.*

PREFERRED WATER DEPTH *Up to 60cm (2ft).*

RECOMMENDED POND SIZE *Medium to large.*

● Pickerel weed (*Pontaderia cordata*)

A rather ugly name for a glorious plant that is thought of as being both a hardy herbaceous plant and a shallow or deep water aquatic. Sited in groups in deeper water, the plants are quite undemanding and come into their own when most other flowers have finished. Often regarded as the best blue-flowered aquatic plant.

FLOWERS *Tiny, pale blue to purple, massed tightly on cylindrical spikes; mid-summer to early autumn. Not all of the flowers on a spike open at the same time, which can give the individual spike a 'moth-eaten' look. But when grown in sufficient numbers, there is a very splendid mass effect of blue flowers.*

LEAVES *Deciduous, deep green, spear- or heart-shaped leaves on strong stalks rising from the water.*

CULTIVATION *Set out pontederia in spring, by planting young plants 30cm (12in) apart, in small isolated groups directly into soil, or in baskets (to limit their spread). They perform well in full sun, but with light shade they have a longer flowering period. Remove dead foliage as it appears.*

HARDINESS *Hardy. Plants survive the winter, so long as the crowns are below the ice. If grown in soil at the pond edge, protect the crowns in winter with a mulch of bracken or straw.*

PROPAGATION *In autumn, sow the fresh seeds in submerged pots under glass. Alternatively, divide mature plants in late spring.*

ORIGINS *It is a native of North America, and is called the 'pickerel' weed after the fact that various types of pike hide in amongst its dense growth in the wild.*

The pale blue flowers of the commonly seen pickerel weed (Pontaderia cordata)

The white-flowered pickerel weed (Pontaderia cordata alba)

HEIGHT *Up to 75cm (30in) above the water line.*
SPREAD *45cm (18in) per year.*
MINIMUM WATER DEPTH *10–38cm (4–15in).*
RECOMMENDED POND SIZE *To maximize the appreciation of this plant, several should be grown. Therefore the best size of pond is medium to large. Not recommended for water barrels, sinks or the like.*
ALTERNATIVE PLANTS *The white-flowered form is worth growing; look for P. cordata alba. Also, the variety P. cordata lancifolia has slimmer leaves, and is a slightly taller plant.*
EXPERT ADVICE *Although pontaderia is perfectly acceptable for growing as a marginal plant, it can become invasive and troublesome. So, many experienced gardeners prefer to treat them as deeper water aquatics, where they can be grown and 'controlled' in planting baskets.*

● Water fringe (*Nymphoides peltata*)

Very pretty almost buttercup-like flowers are held on stems over attractive leathery leaves, making the whole effect similar to small waterlilies. In fact, some gardeners still refer to this as the 'poor man's waterlily'.

FLOWERS *The yellow blooms appear from mid-summer to early autumn. Each flower is 5cm (2in) across, and each petal has a frilled edge, giving it some distinction.*
LEAVES *Heart-shaped, waxy, deciduous leaves 10cm (4in) across, float on the surface of the water. The leaves are slightly mottled light and dark green, with purple undersides.*
CULTIVATION *In spring plant rhizomes or young plants – and unless you have a very large pond, make sure you contain them within planting baskets. This is an invasive plant. Cut off and remove dead foliage in autumn, before it sinks and pollutes the water. Aphids represent the worst pest; wash them off with small jets of water.*
HARDINESS *Very hardy, tolerating temperatures as low as -20°C.*
PROPAGATION *In spring, lift plants out of the pond and divide them.*
ORIGINS *Europe and Asia, and now naturalised in North America.*
HEIGHT *Up to 10cm (4in) above water.*
SPREAD *Up to 60cm (2ft) in each direction after two years.*
PREFERRED WATER DEPTH *To 45cm (18in).*
RECOMMENDED POND SIZE *Medium to large.*
ALTERNATIVE PLANTS *Alternative common names for this*

The pretty buttercup flowers of the water fringe

plant are the fringed waterlily, and the yellow floating heart. Normally only the straight species is seen, but the form 'Bennettii' is becoming more widely available. It produces slightly larger flowers but lacks some of the attractive leaf mottling of the species.

● Water Hawthorn (*Aponogeton distachyos*)

The water hawthorn is an excellent plant for deep water ponds. It is easy to grow and it's very long-flowering, especially when grown in shade. It has attractive floating leaves that are more or less evergreen; and the vanilla-like fragrance of the blooms is powerful and lingering. After the main spring crop of blooms, plants generally collapse

Facts & Figures 27

A South African cookery book recommends the use of water hawthorn flowers for flavouring certain meat dishes, and some people consider the tubers to be edible.

The water hawthorn (Aponogeton distachyos) has a long season of flowers – especially in the shade

until late summer, when they often disappear from sight altogether, unless growing in the shade. By mid-autumn, however, they have usually produced a fresh set of leaves and start flowering again, sometimes through to early winter in mild parts.

FLOWERS *Late spring and again in autumn, or continuously in light shade. Soft white with waxy petals and jet black anthers, in forked spikes that almost float on the surface of the water. Strongly fragrant.*

LEAVES *Oval, long, and mid-green with brown blotches, floating on the surface of the water. Evergreen in mild parts.*

CULTIVATION *Set out water hawthorns in spring, by planting the tubers – or young plants – 45cm (18in) apart, in small isolated groups in baskets, or directly into soil. They perform well in full sun, but with*

light shade they have a longer flowering period. Remove dead foliage as it appears.

HARDINESS *Hardy. Plants survive the winter, so long as the tubers are below the ice.*

PROPAGATION *The freely produced green seeds can be found floating on the surface of the pond during late summer and autumn. Net some ripe seeds, and sow them straight away in containers of water indoors. Alternatively, divide mature plants in late spring.*

ORIGINS *The water hawthorn is a native of the southern tip of the African continent, and has not acclimatized to our more temperate flowering seasons, which is why it produces two flushes of flowers per year.*

HEIGHT *Approx. 10cm (4in) above water.*

SPREAD *60cm (2ft) per year.*

PREFERRED WATER DEPTH *30–90cm (12–36in).*

RECOMMENDED POND SIZE *Tiny: even a water barrel could sustain a plant or two.*

ALTERNATIVE NAME *Sometimes referred to as the Cape pondweed, and is often seen as* A. distachyus. *A yellow-flowered, more tender species is sometimes available; look for* A. desertorum *(also sold as* A. kraussianum).

EXPERT ADVICE *Watch out for snails. They can be very destructive to the leaves, and young plants are particularly at risk.*

Facts & Figures 28

The fleur-de-lis is based upon the iris flower – many believe it to be the yellow flag iris (Iris pseudacorus)

Pinkish heads of willow grass (Persicaria amphibia)

● Willow grass (*Persicaria amphibia*)

A not-too-often seen plant, but one worth searching for from specialist nurseries. Persicaria is the new name for many of the polygonum species, and polygonums are infamous for their rapid growth rate (as in the mile-a-minute vine, *Polygonum baldschuanicum*) and potential as weeds (such as the devastating Japanese knotweed, *P. japonicum*). This particular plant is, as the Latin species name suggests, amphibious: it will grow on land and in water. On land it is as rampant as many of its contemporaries. In the water it is altogether more submissive.

FLOWERS *Tiny pinkish or reddish heads appear on spikes from mid-summer to mid-autumn.*

LEAVES *Elongated, oval, mid-green and deciduous. In deepish water they float, whilst in shallow waters the leaves may point upwards, although never vertical.*

CULTIVATION *Set out young plants in spring, either in planting baskets, or directly into soil. Aphids and leaf spots can occur; wash off the former with jets of water, and remove leaves affected by the latter. Remove dead foliage at any time.*

HARDINESS *Very hardy, tolerating temperatures as low as -20˚C.*

Facts & Figures 29

Nuphar lutea produces very distinctive flask-shaped fruits, as well as its bright yellow flowers, and these are the reason some people refer to it as the 'brandy bottle lily'.

PROPAGATION *Divide the plants in spring, or sow fresh seeds into mud in submerged pots.*

ORIGINS *Throughout the temperate regions of the northern hemisphere.*

HEIGHT *Up to 15cm (6in) above water.*

SPREAD *Up to 60cm (2ft).*

PREFERRED WATER DEPTH *45cm (18in) – the more shallow the water, the more invasive the plant becomes.*

RECOMMENDED POND SIZE *Medium.*

ALTERNATIVE NAME *This plant may be sold under its older name of* Polygonum amphibium, *and may be referred to by its alternative common name, amphibious bistort.*

● Yellow pond lily (*Nuphar lutea*)

Compared with waterlilies, species of nuphar are very vigorous and therefore invasive. They are suited only to large, deep ponds or lakes. However, if these are the sort of conditions you can provide, then nuphars are an excellent choice.

The yellow pond lily (Nuphar lutea)

FLOWERS *Bright yellow cup-shaped flowers, with an odd cat-like scent (although you can't usually get that close), appear in summer.*

LEAVES *This plant offers two entirely different sorts of leaves: rounded, heart-shaped floating leaves up to 30cm (12in) across, and translucent, feathery, thin leaves under the water.*

CULTIVATION *In spring, set out rhizomes or young plants, into baskets (the larger the better). Little attention need be given after this, other than to remove dead foliage or flowers, and to wash off any aphids which dare to make an appearance.*

The sacred lotus (Nelumbo nucifera) *from Asia is a giant of a plant*

HARDINESS *Very hardy, tolerating temperatures as low as -20˚C.*

PROPAGATION *Divide plants in spring.*

ORIGINS *Eastern United States and the West Indies, across to north Africa and into eastern Europe and Asia.*

HEIGHT *Up to 15cm (6in) above water.*

SPREAD *Up to 2m (6ft) in all directions after two years.*

PREFERRED WATER DEPTH *1–2.5m (3–8ft).*

RECOMMENDED POND SIZE *Large – some experts maintain that this plant should not be recommended for a garden pond because of its invasiveness. It's a good lake plant, however!*

ALTERNATIVE PLANTS Nuphar japonica *var.* variegata *and* N. pumila variegata *are much smaller, thriving in a depth of up to 45cm (18in).*

LOTUS BLOSSOM

Where water is the focal point it is fun, and wholly appropriate, to grow a lotus. There are two species of this well-known plant, the hardiest of which is the North American chinkapin (*Nelumbo lutea*). It is the smaller of the two as well, growing to 2m (6ft) in height, with large and showy yellow blossoms. Although not often grown outside in cooler climates, it is reasonably hardy and should produce plenty of typical plate-like foliage if not many flowers.

The sacred lotus (*N. nucifera*) of Asia is a giant of a plant in its original form, but one which has given us a wide range of dwarf cultivars. Try the white, pink-edged 'Chawan Basu' or the carmine-pink 'Pekinensis Rubra', but instead of growing them in the pool try them in a large tub or decorated container at the waterside. When container grown they can be easily moved indoors during the autumn for overwintering in a frost-free place.

WATER IRISES

There are many irises associated with water gardening, and whereas most will only tolerate damp soil conditions, those listed below are very happy growing in a pond with around 10cm (4in) of water over the soil.

Iris pseudacorus

When we moved to our current house about 12 years ago, the pond, which was a simple rectangle sunk into a wide patio, contained four goldfish. Or

A white form of the sacred lotus

The pink sacred lotus needs winter protection

Iris pseudacorus *'Bastardii'*

so we thought. When we transferred the contents to a new pond in a strategically better part of the garden, we discovered over 50 small goldfish and tiddlers. The reason they had avoided discovery was that they had hidden in amongst the roots of an enormous clump of yellow flag iris, *Iris pseudacorus*. The water level, when the mass of roots was removed, went down by two thirds!

What I learnt from that experience, apart from how heavy a big clump of iris root can be, is that irises can be very prolific, and certainly worth a place in the garden. The yellow flag, a native plant to Britain, is the most common of water irises, and roots of it will grow most vigorously. It will, within reason, grow in any depth of water, and I have been known to cruelly chop up small sections with leaves and weigh them down in 37cm (15in) of water, with highly successful results. Just remember to divide your plants every couple of years for the best results.

The species is strong growing with large golden flowers and brown signal flashes, it needs a lot of room in which to grow, so should only be planted into a medium to large pond. There are a number of excellent varieties. One of the most popular is 'Tangawaray Cream', from New Zealand. It has a lovely pale cream flower with brown signals. 'Wychwood Multifloral' is a seedling from 'Tangawaray Cream', with rich golden flowers but with twice the amount of flowering buds as the original.

'Flore Plena' is a hose-in-hose iris, which means that the flower is constructed from many blooms, each one growing inside another.

The form 'Variegata' has golden flowers with deep yellow and green variegated leaves. The actual variegation is not stable; meaning that the flag reverts to green in late summer, but in the following spring it will once again emerge with wonderful bright yellow and green colourings.

Iris pseudacorus *'Variegata'*

There is a stronger growing iris called 'Turnip Seed'. The flag on this plant is extremely strong, quite able to reach a height of 2m (6ft), with large golden yellow flowers.

More diminutive are 'Golden Queen', a completely golden iris with no brown signal flashes, and *Iris pseudacorus* 'Bastardii', a cream variety with pale brown signals. For something completely different you could always try 'Ecru', an almost white flower with dark brown signals. Even smaller than the above, reaching a height of just 60cm (2ft), are 'Dwarf Form', a complete copy of the original iris, but much shorter in stature; 'Alba', a pale creamy white form with brown signals; and finally 'Holden Clough' and 'Ray Davidson'. Both have golden yellow flowers, heavily veined with brown down the whole of the petal, making the flower look extremely dark and inviting.

LEFT: The yellow flag (Iris pseudacorus) *is the most common of water irises*

Iris laevigata

The most important iris for growing in water has to be *I. laevigata*, the Japanese water iris. The Japanese connection is most profound, as the plants originated there, and have been used throughout the centuries in oriental literature and iconography. This iris has become accepted by the West as a symbol of elegance and peace.

The three-petalled blooms of straight *I. laevigata* are about 12.5cm (5in) across, and are borne on 60cm (2ft) high stems – the first flowers opening in early summer, and are a clear blue-violet with a yellow line down the centre of each petal. If plants are enjoying life in the right conditions, a second flush of flowers may appear in late summer or early autumn. There are many dozens of varieties worth considering, but here are my favourites:

The single white version is called 'Alba'. 'Flore Plena' is a double-flowered version of the species and 'Snowdrift' is a double version of 'Alba'.

White flowers with pale mauve mottling at the base of the petals describes 'Mottled Beauty' and the six-petalled double version is called 'Monstrosa'. 'Elegante' has white flowers with heavy dark blue edging, and the double-flowered version is 'Colchesterensis' (sometimes seen as 'Colchesteri').

The three most stunning forms are 'Weymouth' (single), 'Weymouth Midnight' (double) and 'Regal'. The first two are dark blue with pure white signals, and the third is a deep cyclamen-red flower with white signals.

'Variegata' has a wonderful pale blue single flower with a green and white variegated flag. Unlike *Iris pseudacorus* 'Variegata', this iris is stable in colour with wonderful green and white leaves throughout the summer months.

Iris versicolor

This plant, curiously referred to as the American blue flag, actually has a bright green flag with a profusion of small flowers. Its flower stalks are 45–60cm (18–24in) high, the leaves reaching a little higher still. It can come in various colours, the norm being pale blue, through to darker blue, but there are white forms as well as many named varieties. One of these varieties is 'Kermesina', a deep wine red with golden signals. 'Mysterious Monique' has deep red flowers that almost verge to purple. There are also heavily veined varieties: 'Between the Lines' is pure white with pale blue

'Golden Queen' is a deep yellow, slightly smaller cultivar of flag iris

veining throughout, and 'Candy Striper' is a pale cream with medium blue heavy veins.

Louisiana irises

These are naturally distributed in the warm and wet lands of south Louisiana in the United States. *Iris fulva* and *I.* x *fulvala* are just two, and are perhaps the best. They have totally different qualities. The former is pale brown-red, whilst the latter is much showier, with large rich purple flowers and golden signals. Both produce lush green foliage very early in the spring, giving the pond a luxuriant, green effect before much of the other garden foliage has emerged.

There are many Louisiana hybrids being bred at the moment, particularly in North America, and these are something to look forward to. They have so far produced some stunning results, with flowers of pale pink, white, red, yellow, blue and purple, some with ruffled edges and others so double that they look more like a camellia than an iris.

Water irises: technical terms

RHIZOME: this is the root of the plant, which should be planted into good quality topsoil in a planting basket. The rhizome will grow and split into multiple plants, which after a few years can be divided up in the early spring and re-potted into fresh soil and containers.

THE FLAG: the green leaf part of the plant, seen for most of the year. There are many variegated irises which have the flag part coloured by either yellow, cream or white as well as the normal green.

THE FLOWER: probably the most welcome part of the iris. Nearly all of the water irises are bi-annual flowering, meaning each individual plant only flowers every other year, but when they have grown for a few years and you have a clump of them established you will have flowers every year. There are many forms of flowers: single flowers have three petals and three upright standards (almost petals). The petals have what is known as a signal flash in the centre near the stem, which can be of various colours. Double flowers have six petals – the standards have actually become petals. There are also multi-petalled irises, which are mutations with more than six petals.

Guide to growing water irises

SITE *Full sun is preferable; light shade is acceptable.*

SOIL *Newly bought containerized plants will be growing in a suitable soil, but if you are replanting, use good, clean garden soil from a part of the garden that has not recently been dressed with fertilizer. Remove twigs, weeds, old leaves or anything likely to decay and foul the water.*

PLANTING *Do this between mid-spring and mid-summer.*

AFTERCARE *Little is needed once plants are established. Remove dead or scrappy leaves when seen. Dead flower heads should be moved before they set seed (unless you want to collect the seed).*

DIVISION *Most varieties will benefit from lifting and dividing every three or four years. This should take place during mid- to late spring. Use garden soil as described above and plant the offshoots in a new aquatic pot, placing gravel or small stones over the compost to prevent fish disturbing it.*

PESTS AND DISEASES *Aphids, caterpillars and earwigs, are the main pests, while there are several plant viruses which can affect flowering and leaf production. Chemical controls are not possible, so the pests should be washed off and allowed to sink or*

The pale brown-red of Iris fulva

One of the best of the small waterlilies is 'Froebelii' – ideal for growing in a large container

swim! With the remaining problems, the only advice is to gently cut away the affected parts, and to dispose of them. Thankfully these problems are not generally life-threatening.

WATERLILIES

Of all the aquatic plants that grow in our ponds, it is the waterlily that epitomizes the subject to many people. To my mind there are few plants – aquatic or land-based – to compare with the pure exotic pleasure that a succession of waterlily flowers can bring.

Fortunately for waterliliophiles like me, there are plenty of varieties to choose from; the sad thing is that the majority of them grow too big for the small ponds that most of us possess today. It is for this reason that in the early 1900s the French hybridist Latour-Marliac, amongst others, devoted

himself to the creation of newer and better miniature or dwarf varieties, many of which are classed under the category known as the Pygmaea hybrids. Tragically, he took much of his cross-breeding data with him to his grave, but at least he left us with a fabulous range of small and compact varieties, even if the plant parentage of most of them is not fully known.

The pygmy waterlilies are excellent for sinks, troughs or ponds where the water is no deeper than 30cm (12in). Most will grow contentedly in just 10cm (4in) of water, or even in the deeper marginal shelves of a larger pond.

There are really just two notes of caution when it comes to growing these small and compact varieties. The first concerns the likelihood of the plants freezing in winter: despite being hardy, the plants grow in very shallow water which, in the

Flowers of 'Paul Hariot' start yellow and turn reddish-orange as they age

harshest of winters, can freeze solid. The plants should, therefore, be provided with sufficient depth to ensure that the rhizomes remain unfrozen during the coldest spells. If this is not possible, they should be protected, either by draining the pool in autumn, and then covering the lily with thick straw, or by lifting the plant in mid-autumn and keeping it in water in a frost-free place until planting time again.

The second warning is not so serious for the plant, but by ignoring it you could be forfeiting some excellent colour, with resultant substandard plants. Small waterlilies are perfect for growing in contained water features, such as a barrel, tub or sink, but there is a temptation for many of us to fit a small ornamental fountain, or a regular drip-drip feature of some kind. All waterlilies, of whatever size, dislike moving water around their leaves and stems (which suppresses flowering), and this problem can be exacerbated in a container.

'Small' waterlilies

These varieties are ideal for small ponds, or even container water features, with a water depth of 10–30cm (4–12in). They generally have a spread, when mature, of some 30–60cm (1–2ft).

'Aurora' *(yellow, gradually changing through orange to red, semi-double, yellow stamens, mid-green leaves with mottled and marbled patterns)*

'Froebelii' *(vivid red, single, yellow stamens, mid-green leaves)*

'Graziella' *(coppery-red, single, orange stamens, pale green leaves with purple flecking)*

'Johann Pring' *(deep pink, single, stamens in two rings – the inner ones pale orange and the outer ones deep pink – dark green leaves)*

'Maurice Laydeker' *(wine red with white flecks on the outer petals, yellow stamens, single)*

'Paul Hariot' *(yellow, turning reddish-orange, semi-double, fragrant, yellow stamens, mid-green leaves with purplish flecking)*

'Pygmaea Alba' *(also sold as* Nymphaea tetragona; *white, single, golden yellow stamens, dark green leaves, dark red beneath, very tiny indeed – almost the only waterlily that can be grown in an aquarium*

'Pygmaea Rubis' *(wine red, with yellow stamens, single, slightly larger than 'Pygmaea Rubra')*

'Comanche' is a compact waterlily offering a great variety of leaf and flower colour

'Pygmaea Rubra' *(blood red, orange stamens, single, purplish-green leaves with reddish undersides)*

N. x helvola *(canary yellow, single, orange stamens, olive green leaves, mottled with purple and brown)*

'Compact' waterlilies

These are ideal for small ponds, or large contained water features, with a water depth of 30–60cm (1–2ft). They generally have a spread, when mature, of some 60–90cm (2–3ft).

'Albatross' *(pure white, single, golden stamens, purplish leaves, gradually turning deep green)*

'Brakeleyi Rosea' *(fragrant, rose pink fading to flesh and almost white, semi-double, pink stamens, dark green leaves)*

'Comanche' *(small, deep orange changing to bronze with age, semi-double, orange-red stamens, purple leaves, turning green)*

'Ellisiana' *(wine red, gradually darkening, single, orange stamens, mid-green leaves)*

'Firecrest' *(pink, semi-double, fragrant, orange stamens with red tips, green-bronze leaves)*

'Indiana' *(orange-red, ageing to deep red, semi-double, yellow stamens, olive green leaves with darker mottling)*

'James Brydon' *(one of the most widely seen waterlilies,*

*crimson, semi-double to double, fragrant, red
    stamens with gold tips, dark purple-green leaves with
    maroon flecks)*
'Laydekeri Fulgens' *(bright crimson, single, red
    stamens, dark green leaves with purple-brown flecks)*
'Laydekeri Lilacea' *(lilac-pink, single, bright yellow
    stamens, green leaves with a few brown flecks)*
'Laydekeri Purpurata' *(wine-red, single, orange
    stamens, long season of flowering, mid-green leaves
    with purple flecks)*
'Odorata Sulphurea Grandiflora' *(yellow, semi-double,
    yellow stamens, mid-green leaves with brownish
    markings)*
'Robinsoniana' *(orange-red, semi-double, yellow
    stamens, dark green leaves with darker flecking)*
'Rose Arey' *(rose pink, semi-double, fragrant, orange
    stamens, purple leaves, gradually turning green)*
'Sioux' *(yellow, turning orange then rich red, semi-
    double, yellow stamens, greenish bronze leaves with
    brown mottling)*
'Solfatare' *(yellow, turning orange-yellow and then
    red, single, yellow stamens, dark green leaves with
    purple blotches and spots)*

'Larger' waterlilies
Perhaps the most dramatic of all waterlilies are

Nymphaea *'Odorata Sulphurea Grandiflora'* has
showy lemon yellow blooms

the larger cultivars which are more suited, by
definition, to larger ponds – or even lakes. These
require a planting depth of 45–80cm (18–32in),
and produce a spread of leaves, when mature, of
up to 2.4m (8ft).
'Conqueror' *(a good, deep red with white flecks; semi-
    double, yellow stamens, masses of flowers)*
'Escarboucle' *(crimson, red stamens, semi-double,
    fragrant)*
'Gladstoniana' *(white, golden-yellow stamens, double,
    fragrant)*
'Gonnère' *(pink, golden stamens, double)*
'Mrs Richmond' *(pale pink turning to red, yellow
    stamens, double)*

Guide to growing waterlilies
SITE *Full sun is preferable; plants in water barrels and
    the like can be left in partial shade where the water
    won't heat up and cool down quite so rapidly.*
SOIL *Newly bought containerized plants will be
    growing in a suitable soil, but if you are replanting,
    use good, clean garden soil from a part of the garden
    that has not recently been dressed with fertilizer.
    Remove twigs, weeds, old leaves or anything likely to
    decay and foul the water.*
PLANTING *This should take place between mid-spring
    and mid-summer. Newly bought containerized plants
    can be sited straight away, at the appropriate depth for
    the variety. See below for planting divided offshoots.*
AFTERCARE *Little is needed once plants are established.
    Remove dead or scrappy leaves when seen. Dead
    flower heads should be removed before they sink.*
DIVISION *Most varieties will benefit from lifting and
    dividing every three or four years. This should take
    place during mid- to late spring. If the flowers rise on
    their stalks well above the leaves (and they are not
    the tropical species for which this is normal), or if the
    leaves are being supported by other leaves and are
    not laying flat on the surface of the water, it is a
    reasonably good indication that the plant is congested
    and in need of dividing. Use garden soil as described
    above and plant the offshoots in a new aquatic pot,
    placing gravel or small stones over the compost to
    prevent fish disturbing it.*
PESTS AND DISEASES *Aphids (blackfly), waterlily
    beetle, leaf miners, root and rhizome rot and leaf
    spots, are the main problems. As for the water iris
    information above, chemical controls are not
    possible, so wash off the pests and be vigilant over
    the other troubles.*

'Escarboucle' is one of the deepest of crimson waterlilies

'Gladstoniana' is pure white, double, and pleasantly fragrant

CHAPTER 7

MARGINAL PLANTS

Much debate has taken place over the years as to the true definition of a marginal plant. Is it a plant that permanently has its roots in soil under water? Or perhaps a plant that has roots in permanently moist soil? Or maybe even one that has its roots in soil that is wet or under water, but which also has periods of being dry – perhaps during summer? These descriptions confuse even me, so how the poor, beleaguered novice will fair I couldn't say.

My definition of a marginal plant may fly in the face of botanical purists, but at least it is unequivocal as far as the average (and beginner) gardener is concerned: a 'marginal', to my mind, is any plant that grows at the very edge of the water, regardless of the moisture content of the soil in which it's growing. This means that the marginals discussed in this chapter will require a wide range of habitats, spanning all soil conditions, from permanently under water to semi-dry. If we are not careful, however, marginal plants will graduate, almost imperceptibly, into bog garden plants – the subject of our next chapter.

MARGINAL PLANTS

Here are some of the most notable marginals:

● Arrow arum (*Peltandra undulata*)
This hardy, semi-evergreen perennial plant is what we call 'architectural', in that it has good form and structure. Although individual plants are not particularly big, they do look best when planted in large groups. For this reason, they are best suited to larger ponds. Set plants 30cm (12in) apart.

FLOWERS *In early summer, tiny greenish flowers on a short spike enclosed by a conspicuous greenish white spathe, appear. Green berries follow.*
LEAVES *The foliage is bright green, shiny and arrow-shaped. When grown in deeper water, this plant tends to be evergreen.*
CULTIVATION *Set plants out during spring in full sun or very light shade. Plant directly into the soil. Remove any faded foliage in late autumn. Some winter protection of plants not under water, by packing straw or bracken around the crowns, would be advantageous.*

*The arrow arum (*Peltandra undulata*) looks best when planted in large groups*

The elegant arrow-shaped leaves of Sagittaria sagittifolia *are very distinctive*

HARDINESS *Hardy, tolerating temperatures down to -15°C.*

PROPAGATION *Divide the creeping rhizomes in spring.*

ORIGINS *North America.*

HEIGHT *Up to 60m (2ft).*

SPREAD *Up to 45cm (18in).*

PREFERRED WATER DEPTH *0–25cm (0–10in).*

RECOMMENDED POND SIZE *Medium to large.*

ALTERNATIVE PLANTS *This plant may also be found under its old name of* Peltandra virginica*). The white arrow arum (*P. sagittifolia*, or sometimes seen as* P. alba*) has flowers of a purer white, with red berries following.*

● **Arrowhead (*Sagittaria sagittifolia*)**

The leaves of this marginal plant are quite distinctive and, when combined with the flowers – particularly on the double form – make this highly desirable.

FLOWERS *From mid- to late summer fairly large spikes of white flowers with black and red centres are produced. The male flowers are at the tops of the spikes and females below.*

LEAVES *Elegant arrow-shaped leaves are held above the water, whilst long ribbons of leaves are produced under water.*

CULTIVATION *Grow in full sun or light shade. When growing more than one plant, set them out 23cm*

Facts & Figures 30

The arrowhead (*Sagittaria sagittifolia*) has edible roots. It is sometimes referred to as the duck potato because, allegedly, in large duckponds, the feathery inhabitants will attack and eat the tubers.

(9in) apart. Young plants can be planted directly into the soil. Alternatively, you can plant the tubers by weighing them down and dropping them into the water at the pond's edge. Cut back all growth in the autumn. Aphids can be a problem in summer, so wash them off with jets of water.

HARDINESS *Will survive in temperatures as low as -20°C.*

PROPAGATION *Every second or third year, divide and replant when they get overcrowded. Do this in spring. Also, seeds can be sown under glass in spring.*

ORIGINS *UK and Northern Europe.*

HEIGHT *Up to 60m (2ft).*

SPREAD *Up to 45cm (18in).*

PREFERRED WATER DEPTH *5–30cm (2–12in); the deeper the water, the fewer the flowers.*

RECOMMENDED POND SIZE *Medium to large.*

ALTERNATIVE PLANTS *The old botanical name for this plant is* Sagittaria japonica, *and may still be found under this name in some nurseries. The form* S. latifolia *is similar but less hardy, whilst* S. sagittifolia *'Flore Pleno' produces double flowers.*

● Arum lily (*Zantedeschia aethiopica*)

This plant is, perhaps, as well known as a pot plant as it is for growing outside at the margins of a pond. It is quite a hardy subject, as long as its crowns are protected in winter by a mulch of straw or bracken – or by at least 15cm (6in) of water. It is a highly variable plant, impossible to say with absolute conviction that it is either hardy or half-hardy, deciduous or semi-evergreen or, when it comes down to it, whether it is best as a marginal or a bog garden plant. One thing is certain, however. When in full bloom, a large clump can be stunning.

FLOWERS *In spring and summer minute flowers congregate on fragrant yellow spikes which come out from the middle of a large white spathes. Orange or yellow berries will often follow.*

LEAVES *The large, leathery deep green leaves, shaped like elongated hearts, are very dramatic.*

Facts & Figures 31

The small flowers of the bog arum (*Calla palustris*) are said to be pollinated by water snails.

ABOVE: The dramatic bloom of the arum lily (Zantedeschia aethiopica)

RIGHT: The bog arum (Calla palustris)

CULTIVATION *Grow in full sun or partial shade, in the damp soil of a bog garden, or at the edge of a pond, in water. Plant in spring.*

HARDINESS *To -10°C.*

PROPAGATION *Divide plants in spring. Flowers produce many seeds which can be sown the following autumn or spring.*

ORIGINS *South Africa.*

HEIGHT *Up to 60cm (2ft).*

SPREAD *Up to 60cm (2ft).*

PREFERRED WATER DEPTH *5–30cm (2–12in).*

RECOMMENDED POND SIZE *Medium.*

ALTERNATIVE PLANTS *It is sometimes referred to as the calla lily, but not to be confused with the bog arum (*Calla palustris*) – see next entry. The variety* Zantedeschia aethiopica *'Crowborough' is hardier than the species.*

● Bog arum (*Calla palustris*)

A wonderful hardy herbaceous perennial that is perfectly at home either as a marginal or a shallow water aquatic. It is ideal for concealing the sides of a pond, its stout rhizomes eventually colonizing the shallows and supporting a lush dense carpet of leaves. Arguably, the autumn berries are even more attractive than the flowers.

FLOWERS *These appear in late spring and early summer. They are tiny and yellow-green, studded on*

Facts & Figures 32

In parts of Asia the rhizomes of the flowering rush (*Butomus umbellatus*) – see page 84 – are baked and eaten. Very nutritious apparently. Meanwhile, in Lapland, the rhizomes of the bog arum (*Calla palustris*) are dried, ground and 'processed' to be used as a kind of flour for baking in 'missebroed'.

a cylindrical spike enclosed by a prominent white funnel-shaped arum-like spathe.

LEAVES *Broadly heart-shaped, glossy rich green and thick, on long stalks growing from strong creeping rhizomes.*

CULTIVATION *Planting in spring, by placing pieces of the rhizomes 23cm (9in) apart directly into wet soil or in baskets. Choose a position in full sun or light shade, in wet soil at the edge of larger ponds, or in shallow water. If planted in baskets, these plants will not spread so rapidly and are easier to keep in check. Cut down dead foliage in autumn and winter.*

*Bog bean (*Menyanthes trifoliata*) produces white or pale pink star-shaped flowers*

Keep the plants healthy by dividing the larger clumps every four or five years.

HARDINESS *Very hardy, tolerating temperatures down to -20°C.*

PROPAGATION *Divide the rhizomes in spring, then either transplant direct or begin growth in trays of mud under glass and then plant out. The berries – which are poisonous – can be sown when ripe in pots of wet soil.*

ORIGINS *Throughout Northern Europe, Siberia and Atlantic North America, but now naturalized in the British Isles.*

HEIGHT *Up to 30cm (12in) when mature.*

SPREAD *Up to 30cm (12in) when mature.*

PREFERRED WATER DEPTH *Bog garden, or water to a depth of 20cm (8in).*

RECOMMENDED POND SIZE *Medium.*

RELATED PLANTS Zantedeschia aethiopica *(formerly* Calla aethiopica *and often referred to as the calla lily), is a close relation, and an extremely valuable marginal and bog garden plant.*

● Bog bean (*Menyanthes trifoliata*)

This plant is best grown as a marginal, but its roots will also creep out into deeper water to grow as an aquatic, where it is less useful. It is not a true 'bean' in the sense that it is in the same family as the runner bean: its leaves resemble those of the broad bean, and that is where any similarity ends.

FLOWERS *White or pale pink star-shaped flowers open between mid-spring and early summer.*

LEAVES *Smooth, shiny and bright green, developing into pointed, oval leaflets.*

CULTIVATION *Plant in full sun or part shade. It grows best in a soil that is slightly acid. Cut down dead stems in autumn.*

HARDINESS *It will tolerate temperatures as low as -20°C.*

PROPAGATION *Divide larger clumps, every four or five years. Do this in spring, cutting the creeping rhizomes into several rooted sections. Alternatively, during late summer sow seeds in pots of wet soil.*

ORIGINS *Northern Europe.*

HEIGHT *Up to 30m (12in).*

SPREAD *Up to 50cm (20in).*

PREFERRED WATER DEPTH *Up to 25cm (10in).*

RECOMMENDED POND SIZE *Medium to large.*

ALTERNATIVE PLANTS *Only this species is available, and it is sometimes referred to as the marsh trefoil.*

Brass buttons (Cotula coronopifolia) *is more often grown as an annual plant*

● Brass buttons (*Cotula coronopifolia*)

This is a pretty little plant, grown either as a short-lived tender perennial (in warmer countries), but more often as an annual plant. Fortunately it usually produces many seeds when the flowers fade, and these help to ensure a further crop of plants for the following year.

FLOWERS *Small, brilliant golden button-shaped blooms appear from late spring to early autumn.*

LEAVES *Fine, shiny and light green; also aromatic.*

CULTIVATION *Grow in full sun. Plant young plants, or transplant self-sown seedlings in late spring.*

HARDINESS *The severest temperatures tolerated by this plant are in the region of -10°C.*

PROPAGATION *Sow seeds under glass in spring, pricking them out into small pots.*

ORIGINS *South Africa and southern Asia.*
HEIGHT *Up to 15m (6in).*
SPREAD *Up to 30cm (12in).*
PREFERRED WATER DEPTH *0–10cm (0–4in).*
RECOMMENDED POND SIZE *Small.*
ALTERNATIVE PLANTS *Normally the species only is available.*

● Cardinal flower (*Lobelia cardinalis*)

This is a red-flowering lobelia, very closely related to the blue annual lobelia so beloved of container gardeners for their showy, overhanging flower cascades. This plant is different in almost every respect, but mainly in that it is hardier, taller, and not blue. Although many gardeners are tempted to grow this gem in ordinary garden soil, it really only ever performs at its best when it has its roots under water.

FLOWERS *During late summer and early autumn bright, rich-red flowers appear in clusters on tall stalks.*
LEAVES *The foliage is shiny, narrow and reddish-green.*

The cardinal flower (Lobelia cardinalis) *throws up spikes of bright red flowers in summer*

> ## Facts & Figures 33
> If the 'cotton wool' spikes of the cotton grass (*Eriophorum angustifolium*) are picked when at their best, they dry and last well for floral decoration indoors.

CULTIVATION *The best place to plant this lobelia is in full sun or light shade, preferably in shallow water, but it will perform reasonably well in a moist bog garden soil. If you live in a cold part of the country, it would be as well to plant it in a container, and take it to a frost-free greenhouse for winter. Cut down all top growth in autumn and, if sited in a bog garden, cover the crowns with straw or bracken to protect them from the worst of the winter frost. Slugs can be a problem to young growths in spring and early summer.*
HARDINESS *Will tolerate temperatures only as low as -10°C.*
PROPAGATION *Sow seeds under glass, or divide plants: both carried out during spring. Alternatively, take soft cuttings of the plants during summer.*
ORIGINS *North America.*
HEIGHT *Up to 1m (3ft).*
SPREAD *Up to 30cm (12in).*
PREFERRED WATER DEPTH *5–15cm (2–6in).*
RECOMMENDED POND SIZE *Small – even large water container features can house a single plant.*
ALTERNATIVE PLANTS Lobelia fulgens *is larger and more graceful, but marginally less hardy.* Lobelia dortmanna *is a rosette-forming aquatic species, whilst L. siphilitica is a very hardy relative with violet-blue flowers. The hybrid 'Queen Victoria' has L. cardinalis as one of its parents, and is stunning, with its blood-red leaves and carmine flowers.*

● Cotton grass (*Eriophorum angustifolium*)

Despite its name this is not a true grass, but a species of hardy perennial sedge. It is an elegant native to high-altitude pools, streams, marshes and moorlands with acid soils. Suited to a bog garden, or the margins of a pond, it is extremely slow-growing, and is quite unmistakable in late summer when its seedheads form cotton wool-like tufts. Although not the easiest of plants to grow in low-altitude water gardens, it is certainly worth trying.

The seed pods accompanied by the silky white hairs of cotton grass (Eriophorum angustifolium)

FLOWERS *These appear in early to mid-spring, and are small with bright yellow anthers. They are followed in summer by brown seed pods enclosing tufts of white silky hairs. Allow the flower stems to die down naturally each year.*

LEAVES *Dark green, long, slim and drooping, in clumps.*

CULTIVATION *Choose a position in full sun or light shade, in wet, peaty, acid soil at the edge of larger ponds, or in shallow water no deeper than 10cm (4in). Plant during spring 23cm (9in) apart directly into wet soil or in baskets. These are undemanding plants, as long as they have acid soil and water. If growing in the bog garden, as opposed to growing in water, mulch in spring (particularly if the soil is likely to dry out), and feed with a general fertilizer in spring while young. Keep the plants healthy by dividing the larger clumps every four or five years. If space permits, cotton grass should be planted in bold 'drifts' at the edge of a wildlife pond to create a natural effect.*

HARDINESS *Very hardy, tolerating temperatures down to -20˚C.*

PROPAGATION *By division of larger clumps in spring; either transplanted direct, or started into growth in trays of mud under glass and then planted out. Alternatively sow seeds in wet ericaceous compost under glass in spring.*

ORIGINS *Throughout the Northern Hemisphere and into the Arctic regions.*

83

Although not a true rush, the flowering rush (Butomus umbellatus) still likes to grow in shallow water

HEIGHT *Up to 45–75cm (18–30in) when mature.*
SPREAD *Up to 30cm (12in) when mature.*
PREFERRED WATER DEPTH *Approx. 20cm (8in).*
RECOMMENDED POND SIZE *Medium.*
ALTERNATIVE PLANTS *The broad-leafed cotton grass (Eriophorum latifolium) is slightly larger and tolerates some lime content in the soil and water, but it seems to have a shorter life-span.*

● Flowering rush (*Butomus umbellatus*)

This not a true rush despite, in some respects, resembling one. It is perfectly at home in the shallow waters of a still pool.

FLOWERS *During mid- to late summer, rose pink blooms are held in rounded heads some 2.5cm (1in) across (see picture above).*

LEAVES *Narrow, grass-like and green or purplish.*
CULTIVATION *Plant in spring in full sun. Cut down all growth in autumn. Sometimes aphids can be a summer problem, but can be washed off by jets of water from a hosepipe.*
HARDINESS *Will survive temperatures as low as -20°C.*
PROPAGATION *Sow seeds under glass in autumn. Divide overgrown clumps every three or four years, in spring.*
ORIGINS *Temperate parts of Asia and Europe, including Britain.*
HEIGHT *Up to 1.5m (5ft).*
SPREAD *Up to 60cm (2ft).*
PREFERRED WATER DEPTH *2.5–15cm (1–6in).*
RECOMMENDED POND SIZE *Medium.*
ALTERNATIVE PLANTS *The white-flowered variety 'Schneeweissen' is excellent.*

The greater spearwort (Ranunculus lingua *'Grandiflorus') is a buttercup with particularly showy flowers*

● Greater spearwort (*Ranunculus lingua* 'Grandiflorus')

Most ranunculus species (buttercups and spearworts) can be fairly invasive, but this marginal beauty redeems itself by having very showy flowers.

FLOWERS *Large, 5cm (2in) across, golden yellow and glistening, from mid-spring to early autumn.*

LEAVES *Long, spear-shaped leaves – hence the common name – of bright green, decidedly pinkish when young.*

CULTIVATION *Choose a spot in full sun or light shade, and plant in spring either directly into the soil,* or into planting baskets for siting on ledges around the pond margins. Remove all of the year's growth at the end of autumn. Mildew may be a problem in late summer and autumn.

HARDINESS *Will survive short periods at -20°C.*

PROPAGATION *Divide overgrown clumps, probably every three to four years, in spring. Sow seeds in to pots of moist compost in spring, and keep them in a shaded cold frame.*

ORIGINS *Throughout Europe and Asia.*

HEIGHT *Up to 1m (3ft).*

SPREAD *Up to 30cm (12in).*

PREFERRED WATER DEPTH *0–10cm (0–4in).*

RECOMMENDED POND SIZE *Medium.*

ALTERNATIVE PLANTS *The lesser spearwort* (Ranunculus flammula) *is less invasive, but not as decorative. This plant can be chosen for a small pond.*

Facts & Figures 34

Houttuynia cordata 'Chameleon' (which can also be found wrongly named as 'Tricolor' or 'Variegata') creates as much dissension with gardeners as it does praise. Its 'unnatural-looking' leaves are, to some, gaudy and unnecessary, whilst to others they are magnificently ornate.

● *Houttuynia cordata* 'Chameleon'

Houttuynia cordata (for which there is no easier-to-pronounce common name), is a vigorous and easily grown semi-evergreen plant for the bog garden or water's edge. It makes attractive ground cover and can become charmingly invasive unless

Houttuynia cordata *'Chameleon' is an attractive water or bog garden plant, which can be invasive*

confined in some way. The form 'Chameleon' outsells any of the other forms and its brightly coloured leaves never fail to make a talking point.

FLOWERS *In early summer small, white flowers appear in cone-shaped spikes. Each has four-petals.*

LEAVES *The real beauty of this plant is in its bold, heart-shaped variegated leaves containing shades of pink, yellow, green, cream and white.*

CULTIVATION *Plant during the spring or autumn, directly into the soil at the edge of the pond, or in baskets to restrain root spread. Houttuynia*

prefers a position in partial shade, but will comfortably tolerate full sun or shade. Planting should be into wet soil, or directly into shallow water – but no deeper than 10cm (4in). There is little maintenance required: remove dead or fading foliage when seen, and a general tidy-up in the autumn. Mulch soil-grown plants with compost in the autumn to protect the roots from frost. Aphids and mildew can pose a few problems, but they are not usually serious. Clumps can grow large, so should be divided every four or five years.

The marsh marigold (Caltha palustris) *has deep buttercup-like flowers and large, rounded leaves*

HARDINESS *Very hardy, tolerating temperatures down to -20°C.*

PROPAGATION *Divide the spreading roots of larger clumps in spring. Gardeners keen to try their propagating skills can sow seed of houttuynia in spring, in a garden frame. Keep the compost moist.*

ORIGINS *Straight* Houttuynia cordata *came originally from the Far East and Asia. 'Chameleon' is a man-made hybrid, introduced within the past 20 years.*

HEIGHT *Up to 30cm (12in) after three or four years.*

SPREAD *Up to 45cm (18in) after three or four years.*

PREFERRED WATER DEPTH *0–10cm (0–4in).*

RECOMMENDED POND SIZE *Small to large. The smallest of ponds can only really accommodate single plants.*

ALTERNATIVE PLANTS *The straight species has mainly green-blue leaves with reddish margins and veining. The form 'Flore Pleno' has double flowers.*

Irises

We have already visited a number of irises for the water garden in Chapter 6. There are many dozens of others that are suited either to the pond margins or the bog garden. As they are fairly interchangeable, I have opted to include them in the latter; they are discussed therefore in Chapter 8.

Kingcup (*Caltha palustris*)

See Marsh Marigold on next page.

Facts & Figures 35

A larger and more vigorous form of the marsh marigold, *Caltha palustris*, is available. As if to emphasize its stature, it is called *Caltha palustris* var. *palustris*.

Unlike most hypericums, the marsh St John's wort (Hypericum elodioides) *is happiest in mud or shallow water*

● Marsh marigold (*Caltha palustris*)

This plant, also referred to as the kingcup, is surely one of the most familiar and loved plants for pondside planting. It is, for want of a better description, a water 'buttercup', with deep golden flowers and large, rounded leaves. Much of the appeal of the plant derives from the neatness of habit: caltha doesn't become straggly and unkempt in the way so many marginals do.

FLOWERS *From mid-spring to early summer, golden yellow, waxy buttercup-like blooms appear, proud of the leaves.*

LEAVES *Glossy, dark green deciduous leaves, that are more or less rounded, are carried on long stalks.*

CULTIVATION *Plant in early spring, directly into the soil at the edge of the pond. Caltha prefers a position in full sun or light to medium shade (it is often found naturally in waterlogged woodland soils). There is little maintenance required: remove dead foliage when seen, and a general tidy-up in the autumn.*

Aphids and mildew can pose a few problems, but they are not usually serious. Clumps can grow large, so should be divided every four or five years.

HARDINESS *Very hardy, tolerating temperatures as low as -20°C.*

PROPAGATION *Sow fresh seed in late summer or early autumn, in wet soil. You can also divide the spreading roots of larger clumps in spring (or wait until late summer).*

ORIGINS *A native British plant, also found in parts of Northern Europe, America, even as far as the Arctic Circle.*

HEIGHT *Up to 60cm (1ft).*

SPREAD *Up to 50cm (20in).*

PREFERRED WATER DEPTH *0–15cm (0–6in).*

RECOMMENDED POND SIZE *Small to medium.*

The smallest of ponds can only really accommodate single plants. If planting directly into soil under water, there should be a maximum water depth of 15cm (6in).

The dainty blue flowers of the water forget-me-not (Myosotis scorpioides) *– see page 92*

ALTERNATIVE PLANTS *Most gardeners tend to grow the single-flowered species. Alternatively there is the tightly double-flowered 'Flore Pleno', which is very free-flowering, or the single-flowered white form, 'Alba' (which is slightly more compact and therefore ideal for smaller ponds).* Caltha leptostyla *is better placed for small ponds. It is smaller than* C. palustris, *with rather dainty star-like, golden-centred white flowers.*

EXPERT TIP *For a more impressive display, plant three or more plants together, about 30cm (12in) apart. Massed planting looks so much better than singles,*

but obviously the size of the pond will dictate whether this is possible.

● Marsh St John's wort (*Hypericum elodioides*)

Most hypericums are showy long-lived shrubs, but this small, creeping relative is happiest in mud or shallow water. It is a good plant for concealing the edges of pond liners.

FLOWERS *Small, yellow trumpet flowers appear at the tips of the stems from mid-summer to early autumn.*

LEAVES *These are small, oval and woolly, pale green to green-grey.*

CULTIVATION *A sunny spot brings out the best in this plant, but it will tolerate light shade. Plant in groups for best effect. Tidy the plants in autumn, removing dead leaves or flowers.*

HARDINESS *Will survive -20°C for short periods.*

PROPAGATION *Divide large clumps every four or five years, in spring. Take cuttings of soft young growth in summer.*

ORIGINS *Western Europe.*

HEIGHT *Up to 30cm (12in).*

SPREAD *Up to 45cm (18in).*

PREFERRED WATER DEPTH *0–8cm (0–3in).*

RECOMMENDED POND SIZE *Small ponds but, it has to be said, this plant is perhaps best as a small contribution to a massed planting around a medium-sized pond or larger.*

ALTERNATIVE PLANTS *This is the only aquatic hypericum, and may be seen under an often-used incorrect name, H. elodes.*

● Musks (*Mimulus* spp.)

There are several musk flowers which make excellent plants for pond edges and margins. They really do need room to grow, because they are fairly invasive and have a propensity to self-seed, so larger water gardens make the best homes.

FLOWERS *Usually yellow, orange, red or lavender blue on tall spikes. Close-up, the blooms have pronounced lips, rather like snapdragons.*

LEAVES *The foliage is deciduous, small, mid-green and rounded.*

LEFT: Leaves of the sweet flag (Acorus calamus) produce a sweet smell when crushed

Facts & Figures 36

One of the garden musks, *Mimulus moschatus*, was in past centuries amongst our most richly perfumed garden flowers. Then, inexplicably, around the year 1914, all of the strains of this plant across the globe lost much of their fragrance – and have never regained it.

Facts & Figures 37

The leaves of the sweet flag, *Acorus calamus*, were used to cover the floors of castles before carpets. The 'sweet' part of the name refers to the pleasing aroma – cinnamon or citrus, depending on one's olfactory prowess – which comes from the leaves when they are crushed. The plant's rhizome also contains an oil that is extracted for use in the perfume industry.

CULTIVATION *All of the musks grow best in full sun. Set out young plants, or transplant self-sown seedlings, in spring. Cut back dead or dying stems in the autumn. Mimulus tend to be pest-free, but may sometimes be vulnerable to rots, such as the grey mould fungus.*

HARDINESS *Will survive temperatures as low as -20°C.*

PROPAGATION *Divide overcrowded plants every two or three years, in spring. Take softwood cuttings in summer. Seed of some forms, such as Mimulus ringens, can be sown in spring.*

ORIGINS *North America.*

HEIGHT *This varies with the species. Most will reach up to 45cm (18in), but both M. lewisii and M. ringens will reach double this.*

SPREAD *Up to 50cm (20in).*

PREFERRED WATER DEPTH *0–8cm (0–3in), but 8–15cm (3–6in) in the case of M. ringens.*

RECOMMENDED POND SIZE *Medium.*

RECOMMENDED PLANTS *The water musk or yellow musk (Mimulus luteus) produces yellow blooms with red blotches during high summer, whilst the blooms of the monkey musk (M. moschatus) are all-over yellow. At the same time the lavender musk (M. ringens) carries bluish flowers. The great purple monkey flower (M. lewisii) carries pink to wine purple flowers from early summer to mid-autumn.*

● Sweet flag (*Acorus calamus*)

This is a popular hardy herbaceous foliage plant which looks like an iris, but is in no way related. Its variegated form is the one most often seen.

FLOWERS *Insignificant, green-brown flowers held on arum-like spikes are carried at the tops of the stems. In warm climates reddish fruits are formed.*

LEAVES *Deciduous, arching, iris-like leaves up to 2.5cm (1in) wide have a very pronounced mid-rib.*

CULTIVATION *Plant rhizomes in spring, directly into the soil. Choose a site that is in full sun or very light shade.*

HARDINESS *Temperatures as low as -20°C will be tolerated.*

PROPAGATION *By division in spring.*

ORIGINS *Asia and North America (although widely naturalized in Europe).*

HEIGHT *Up to 1.2m (4ft).*

SPREAD *Up to 75cm (30in).*

PREFERRED WATER DEPTH *8–25cm (3–10in).*

RECOMMENDED POND SIZE *Small to medium.*

ALTERNATIVE PLANTS Acorus calamus *'Variegatus' produces gold and cream striped leaves, and is slightly smaller.* A. gramineus *(referred to as the Japanese rush, although the plant is not technically a rush) is about half the size of* A. calamus, *and has almost grass-like leaves.*

● Water forget-me-not (*Myosotis scorpioides*)

A common wild plant often found growing on river margins, this is a true and unmistakable forget-me-not, with its jolly blue flowers held on spindly long stems. It is easily grown in most situations, and very reliable. It has creeping rhizomes that are not invasive and will trail into the water, making it an ideal choice for masking pond edges.

FLOWERS *Small, rounded, single flowers of intense azure blue (with a yellow, pink or white eye) appear from mid-spring to mid-summer.*

LEAVES *Small, oval, bright green hairy leaves are carried on long trailing stems. Deciduous.*

CULTIVATION *Plant in spring or autumn in moist soil close to the water's edge. Will tolerate a position equally well in full sun and heavy shade (some even*

Facts & Figures 38

Most mints suffer towards the end of the season with the fungal diseases mildew or rust, or both. Whilst these will also affect water mint, the leaf damage is generally less significant here than on some other garden mints.

say that this plant is the most shade-tolerant of all flowering aquatics). Cut down dead growth in autumn; lift and divide vigorous plants every three years. Watch out for aphids in summer and – just like the garden forget-me-not – mildew towards the end of their annual display. In this case, remove all top growth (leaves and stems) and compost or burn it. Mildew will not kill the plants.

HARDINESS *Extremely hardy, tolerating winter temperatures as low as -20°C.*

PROPAGATION *Divide clumps in spring; separate rooted rhizomes or by transplanting the self-sown seedlings (from species only) in spring.*

ORIGINS *Europe and Asia.*

HEIGHT *Up to 30cm (12in) above water.*

SPREAD *Up to 60cm (2ft); the stems are much longer, but trail down.*

PREFERRED WATER DEPTH *0–15cm (0–6in).*

POND SIZE *From small to lake-size.*

ALTERNATIVE PLANTS *There are several varieties worth growing. 'Semperflorens' is a prolific flowerer and has the longest season of all. It has fewer leaves than the others, and is less likely to look straggly. 'Alba' produces white flowers, valuable in the water garden, but is less robust than the blue forms. Other varieties include 'Pinkie', pink, and 'Mermaid', large bright blue flowers over a long season.*

EXPERT TIP *Grow some of the white forms in amongst the blue for a breathtaking effect.*

● Water mint (*Mentha aquatica*)

A hardy herbaceous perennial, this plant was once one of the most popular of marginal plants for the average garden. Now, mainly because of brighter and better hybridiZed alternatives, the mint is grown mostly in wildlife ponds. Here, it is an indispensable plant for covering the margins, with its aromatic leaves and flowers that attract bees and other foragers. It is so easy to grow that it can soon become invasive.

FLOWERS *These appear in mid- to late summer. They are characteristic of most mints: tiny, pale mauve and fragrant, in tight, round clusters at the ends of shoots. Prior to flowering, leaf and stem growth can be very rapid, and some control may be desirable. Once the flower shoots start to appear, however, this growth slows down.*

LEAVES *Deciduous. Small, oval, woolly/hairy leaves, dark green turning reddish purple in bright sun. Very heavily scented when crushed.*

Water mint (Mentha aquatica) is useful for attracting bees and other insects to the pond area

CULTIVATION *Plant during spring in groups of three or four for impact. Choose a position in full sun, or light to medium shade. If planted in baskets, these plants will not spread so rapidly and are easier to keep in check. Cut down all growth in autumn. Keep the clumps healthy by dividing every three or four years.*

HARDINESS *Very hardy, tolerating temperatures as low as -20°C.*

PROPAGATION *By division in spring; by stem cuttings – exceedingly easy to root – in spring or summer, or by seed, sown in spring.*

ORIGINS *Throughout Europe*

HEIGHT *Up to 1m (3ft) when mature.*

SPREAD *Up to 75cm (30in) when mature.*

PREFERRED WATER DEPTH *15cm (6in).*

RECOMMENDED POND SIZE *Small.*

ALTERNATIVE PLANTS Mentha cervina *is less common, but is slightly daintier; low-growing, it forms leafy clumps with lilac-blue flowers in late summer. Pennyroyal (*M. pulegium*) is closely related; dwarf and sprawling, it also thrives in very wet soil.*

93

CHAPTER 8

BOG GARDEN PLANTS

The bog garden, although not a water garden in the purest form, does have a place in this book: at one end of the bog plant list are those species that like to be almost in the water, and are therefore just slightly removed from the marginals featured in the last chapter; at the other end there are those plants that require merely a consistently moist soil.

As sweeping generalizations go, bog garden plants tend to dislike dry, clay soil which resembles concrete in hot summers, and tend not to perform well if they are in a position exposed to high winds and the full strength of the sun all day long. Other than that, they enjoy a wide and varied selection of growing conditions.

PLANTS FOR THE BOG GARDEN

● *Arum italicum* 'Marmoratum'

This is a woodland plant and has qualities in triplicate. First, the pretty marbled leaves, which provide the longest period of attraction. Second the flowers – greenish spathes, typical of the aroid family of plants – with their white interiors. And third, the autumn colour provided by the yellow spikes, which are topped with clusters of the brightest blood-orange berries. No self-respecting bog garden would be without this gem.

FLOWERS *In spring creamy white spathes appear, held proud over the ground, followed by stout spikes of rich orange-red berries in autumn.*

LEAVES *Glossy, arrow-shaped and marbled with shades of grey, yellow-green, and greenish-white.*

CULTIVATION *A moist, but not waterlogged, soil is preferred. Plant the tubers approximately 15cm (6in) deep, or as young plants up to the soil mark on the stem base. Little care is required once this arum is established, but it is useful if a handful of general fertilizer is applied around the base of the plant in spring. If slugs eat the autumn berries, control them in the same way as for normal (i.e. non-bog) garden plants: apply pellets, traps or gels, to the soil where the beasts are likely to be most troublesome.*

HARDINESS *Will survive temperatures as low as -15°C.*

PROPAGATION *Divide the plants – carefully, because the stem tissue is soft and easily damaged – in spring or autumn. Collect and sow seed: save the fresh, ripe fruits and wash away every trace of berry flesh; sow in a soil-based compost under glass, and be patient, for germination can take several months.*

ORIGINS *England, south-east Europe and the Canary Islands.*

HEIGHT *Up to 55cm (10in).*

SPREAD *Up to 30cm (12in).*

ALTERNATIVE PLANTS *This form may still be found with its old name of* Arum italicum *'Pictum'. The straight species does not have the attractive leaf marbling.*

● Astilbe

These are ubiquitous little plants. I notice them in most gardens I visit – whether or not there are bog gardens – and they are often planted in unsuitably hot, dry and sunny places. But this doesn't really matter, for astilbes are the most accommodating of plants – colourful, easy, dramatic and stately. In all cases they are tough and hardy but, it has to be said, without moisture and shade, they can fall well short of their display potential.

RIGHT: The attractive seed head of
Arum italicum *'Marmoratum'*

Astilbe x *'Bressingham Beauty'*

Astilbe x arendsii *'Fanal'*

FLOWERS *Flowering generally begins in early summer and the attractive plume-like heads of tiny flowers, which last for several weeks, ensure that the astilbe owner has a good return on investment. The rusty-brown seed heads produced in late summer and autumn are almost as effective as the flower spikes.*

LEAVES *From mid-spring onwards the leaves appear and develop, all deeply cut and often purplish or bronzy green.*

CULTIVATION *Moisture is more important than shade, and astilbes should not be allowed to dry out. Rich soil – plenty of compost, with an annual mulch when*

dormant – will go a long way to making good any moisture deficiency. Some shelter from strong winds will also be helpful, as this prolongs the flowering period. Given reasonably constant moisture, an annual mulch and, perhaps, a little dappled shade, plants can be left for years.

HARDINESS *Temperatures as low as -20°C will be tolerated.*

PROPAGATION *They can be divided, without much difficulty, when they're old and dormant.*

ORIGINS *Japan and throughout Asia, also North America.*

HEIGHT *Astilbes vary in height from 10cm (4in) to 2m (6ft), and even the tallest need no staking.*

SPREAD *Up to 60cm (2ft).*

● Varieties

The gardener cannot complain about the lack of choice. The hybrids borne out of *Astilbe* x *arendsii* are the most commonly seen, and these generally will produce plumes up to 1m (3ft) in height. One of my favourites is the bright pink 'Bressingham Beauty', an old stager but nevertheless still one of the best.

The variety 'Fire' is often found under its German name 'Feuer' and, not surprisingly, produces a brilliant red flower head.

RIGHT: The salmon pink blooms of
Astilbe x arendsii *'Bumalda'*

Facts & Figures 39

The roots of astilbes are very thirsty and, in a hot drought, watering overhead can be ineffective. Take several large tins – paint pots or large soup tins are perfect – and sink them between the plants so that the rims come to about an inch below the soil surface. It will be easiest to do this during late winter or early spring, when the plants are dormant. During hot summer weather you will be able to fill the tin with water once a day, and moisture will percolate through. One tin is sufficient for three plants.

Astilbe × arendsii 'White Queen'

Astilbe chinensis 'Intermezzo'

For possibly the purest white arendsii hybrid, go for 'White Queen', but others to be recommended include: 'Amethyst', lilac purple; 'Hyazinth', sugar pink; 'Irrlicht', white with dark leaves; 'Venus', pale pink and slightly taller; 'Federsee', intense salmon pink, and 'Fanal', rich orange-red.

The species *A. simplicifolia* has added its quota to the range of hybrids. The straight type is pretty, with graceful pink spikes 37cm (15in) tall, but the variety 'Atrorosea' is superb, carrying sheaves of tiny bright pink flowers for a long time. There is white in this range, and a charming dark-leafed pink variety only 23cm (9in) high called 'Bronce Elegans'. For this, and the salmon 'Dunkellachs', shade as well as a humus-rich soil is needed.

Happily, 'Sprite' is more adaptable. This has dark leaves which look most effective with the sprays carrying masses of tiny flowers of pale shell pink. 'Sprite' will grow to 30cm (12in), and the same across, making it ideal for the front of the border.

There are a couple of varieties from the species *A. japonica* that are worth mentioning, both growing to about 60cm (2ft). The white 'Deutschland' is regularly used for forcing as pot plants, and 'Etna' carries beautiful rich red plumes above mounded foliage.

'Professor van der Weilen' is a hybrid from the Japanese species *A. thunbergii*. It is a graceful plant, with handsome leaves, topped by arching sprays of creamy white flowers. It is a little taller – at 1.2m (4ft) – and flowers in mid-summer, a bit later than most.

Where height variations are important there should be room for such beauties as *A.chinensis tacquetii* 'Superba'. This grows to a stately 1.5m (5ft) with dark outspanning foliage and

The leaves of bugle (Ajuga reptans) *will trail over a low wall. This is cultivar 'Burgundy Glow'*

noble spikes of bright rosy purple flowers over a lengthy period. 'Intermezzo' is mid-pink and very floriferous.

And finally, there is *A. chinensis pumila*. This has a creeping habit of fresh, crispy leaves, close to the ground. It has stumpy 30cm (12in) spikes of lilac-rose colour, and is less fussy about moisture than most.

● Bugle (*Ajuga reptans*)

This shade-loving ground-cover plant thrives when growing under trees and shrubs, as long as the soil is moderately moist all the time. The greatest irony with ajuga is that the dark-coloured leaves are not seen at their best when the plant is growing in a shady place. Yet if you transfer the plant to a sunnier spot, in order to enjoy its foliage, it sits and sulks and never performs its best. If this is a mystery, however, it is no greater than the one surrounding its common name. Why 'bugle'? I'm not certain anyone knows.

FLOWERS *Short spikes of small, lipped, purple flowers appear in spring.*

LEAVES *Rounded leaves of deep green with reddish-purple tints, more pronounced in the younger leaves.*

CULTIVATION *Give the plants a little general fertilizer in spring, followed by a mulch. Trim the plant back, in autumn, if you need to restrict its spread. Mildew can often be a problem later in the season, but this is not life threatening.*

HARDINESS *Will survive temperatures as low as -20°C.*

PROPAGATION *By division in spring.*

ORIGINS *Northern Europe*

HEIGHT *Up to 15cm (6in).*

SPREAD *Up to 1m (3ft).*

ALTERNATIVE PLANTS *The form 'Alba' has whitish flowers, 'Atropurpurea', purple, with deep purple-bronze leaves; 'Variegata' has deep green leaves with cream margins, whilst 'Burgundy Glow' has claret-coloured leaves. The form 'Multicolor' (which may also be found under the names 'Rainbow' and 'Tricolor') has blue flowers and dark bronze leaves splattered with blotches of pink, red and cream.*

● Day lilies (*Hemerocallis* spp.)

The individual flowers of the day lily do indeed last just one day. They can be grown in any part of the garden, but they perform best in

'Pink Damask' can be seen in a variety of colour ranges, from pink to salmon

reasonably moist soil, which means that they make luxuriant additions to any bog garden. They look fabulous next to a pond, too, and an almost surreal appearance can be achieved when their arching stems are reflected in the clear water of a still pool.

The added appeal of these plants is that they are so easy to grow and propagate. I started 12 years ago with a single plant, and this has been added to with new varieties and divisions since and, if I had the room, I'd grow many more. Growing day lilies is quite infectious!

Day lilies have come in for a great deal of attention in recent years from hybridists in Europe and North America. Growers in the early 1900s, such as George Yeld and Amos Perry, raised many beautiful varieties, but only a handful of these are still available commercially.

However, because of the popularity of these plants, dozens of other hybridists were encouraged to 'have a go', and several thousand named forms have been created. Many have

disappeared from cultivation because they were surpassed in excellence by newer forms. Even so, there are well over 300 varieties available to the gardener today (especially in the USA, where certain sections of the gardening community regard them as cult plants).

FLOWERS *The individual trumpet-shaped flowers are not particularly attractive in their own right, particularly when they are a day old and are on the wane. The real beauty is when you see a mass of flowers. The varieties that produce flowers of a single colour, with the colour repeated on the outside of the trumpet, are far more effective in a border than those that have their main colour concentrated inside the trumpet, as it can then only be seen if the flower is looked at end on. But beware of some of the 'red' varieties – there is no true scarlet or carmine yet available and they can look very scrappy en masse and add nothing to the overall effect of the border. Nearly all the yellow varieties have the bonus of being scented, whereas most of the others are lacking this attribute.*

LEAVES *The arching, rushy leaves are a feature in their own right in spring: they are the brightest of greens, and grow almost an inch a day. At flowering time the leaves complement the trumpet flowers, which come on smooth stems 45–90cm (18–36in) tall.*

CULTIVATION *They can be planted at any time from early autumn to mid-spring. Soil should be enriched in advance and, when fully established, some general fertilizer and mulching in spring will encourage fine flowers. The best site is in full sun or light shade (heavy shade depresses flower production). Most soils are tolerated, but plants are best in fairly rich, loamy soil. Cut dead flower stalks back to the base as soon as the last flowers on them have faded. Cut away all foliage, right back to soil level, in the autumn. If you leave this, it will simply turn to an untidy mess over winter.*

HARDINESS *Very hardy, surviving temperatures as low as -20°C.*

PROPAGATION *Divide plants in autumn or spring. Plants become large and difficult to lift when old and I regularly ignore the rules about 'carefully lifting and gently teasing the roots apart'! Instead, I roughly spade through a clump in situ – either to reduce its size or to obtain sections to plant elsewhere. Such a fearless course has never resulted in harm to the plants, and is certainly easier than digging up a big plant and then dividing it.*

One of the finest day lily hybrids is 'Crimson Icon'

ORIGINS *Many originated in eastern Europe and Asia, but some have been grown in the UK since the sixteenth century. To the average gardener, however, it is the many dozens of modern hybrid forms which offer most range of colour and habit.*
HEIGHT *Up to 1m (3ft).*
SPREAD *Up to 1m (3ft).*

The following are some of the best garden hybrids: 'Orangeman', first bred in 1906, is a gorgeous deep orange. 'Hyperion' was introduced nearly 50 years ago, and is still in demand for its clear colour and large yellow flowers. A newer and outstanding yellow is 'Lark Song'. Then there is 'Black Magic', deep ruby mahogany; 'Contessa', light orange; 'Bonanza', soft yellow but very dwarf, matching well with the deeper coloured

'Golden Chimes', which is also dwarf; and 'Crimson Icon', crimson petals with lemon yellow centre.

'Dubloon' (sometimes sold as 'Golden Orchid') is superb, rich gold and growing to 1m (3ft). 'Nigrette' is mahogany purple; 'Pink Damask' ranges from true pink to salmon; 'Primrose Mascott', pale lemon; 'Stafford', bronzy red; 'Anzac', rich red; 'Luxury Lace', lavender; and 'Stella d'Oro', dwarf yellow.

'Corky' is one of the latest to flower. It has much smaller and more refined blooms than most other hybrids. The petals are yellow with a broad bronze stripe down the reverse of each.

'Catherine Woodberry', pink with yellow markings, is another excellent form, as are 'Hornby Castle', dull brick-red; 'Morocco Red', maroon with a yellow throat; 'Pink Prelude',

Hemerocallis *'Stella d'Oro'*

pink; 'Little Wine Cup', burgundy red with a
yellow throat; 'Cream Drop', with exquisite
small, creamy yellow flowers; 'Buzz Bomb',
deep velvety red; 'Chartreuse Magic', canary
yellow and green; 'Berlin Yellow', good, solid
yellow all over and 'Stoke Poges', pink with
orange markings.

There are only a handful of double-flowered
varieties, and they don't generally add much to
the range. Arguably the best double is *H. fulva*
'Kwanso Flora-Plena', with reddish orange flowers.

The arching early spring foliage of hemerocallis

RECOMMENDED VARIETIES

Although there are several species available, these
tend to be found only in specialists' gardens. The
earliest show colour in late spring, as in the case
of the early and dwarf species *H. dumortierii*,
which has yellow flowers lasting for several
weeks. *H. citrina* and *H. lilioasphodelus* are
charming, fragrant yellow species for late spring
and early summer. Another species, *H. multiflora*,
produces pale orange-yellow flowers in great
profusion from mid-summer to mid-autumn.

● Ferns

Few plants suggest the prehistoric age quite
like the fern and these shade-loving plants
have been around since the dinosaur, which
means that they are sturdy, durable and hardy.

Hemerocallis *'Berlin Yellow'*

'Stoke Poges' is a brightly coloured hemerocallis – pink with orange markings

More often than not they grow in damp places although, it has to be said, a dank atmosphere is as important to them as a wet soil. Indeed, it is quite a common occurrence for the crown and roots of outdoor ferns to rot in very wet soil.

FLOWERS *Ferns do not flower and produce seeds in the conventional sense – they reproduce by means of spores, which are often seen as small brownish pustules on the undersides of the fronds.*

FRONDS *Ferns make up for the lack of colour by boasting a wide variety of frond shapes and sizes, most in varying shades of green.*

CULTIVATION *In spring plant single, specimen plants in full sun, or light to moderate shade. The ideal soil is moist and acid, with plenty of humus. Mulch with garden compost after planting, and annually in spring, and feed with a general fertilizer at the same time. With deciduous ferns it is advisable to protect the emerging young fertile fronds in spring by leaving the dead fronds in place at the end of autumn. Cut these back in spring when the worst of the weather is past, and the new shoots are starting to emerge.*

HARDINESS *They vary, tolerating temperatures from -10°C down to -20°C.*

PROPAGATION *Divide congested clumps in spring but beware – this is not always an easy job, particularly with the larger forms like osmunda. Chopping off a small portion may be all that is possible. Another way of increasing stock of the fern is to surface-sow ripe spores under glass in autumn or spring. But again, beware! Although ferns produce liberal quantities of spores, many have a very short life, their viability being little more than a few days after ripening.*

RECOMMENDED SPECIES *The royal fern (Osmunda regalis) is generally considered to be the best fern for pondside or bog garden planting and it is, arguably, the most impressive of all the hardy deciduous ferns. It was once common in the wild wet fens and marsh banks of Europe, but is now most often seen in*

The royal fern (Osmunda regalis) is one of the best waterside ferns

The sensitive fern (Onoclea sensibilis) *is 'sensitive' to autumn frosts*

gardens. It is a highly desirable plant for large pond and streamside situations, and is very vigorous and spreading, although some of the cultivated forms are less demanding of space. The lime green, prettily divided fronds first appear as copper-tinted crooked shoots in spring, and finally turn yellow and bronze in autumn. Smaller, stiffer, spore-bearing fronds arise from the centre of the plant. Closely related forms include O. regalis 'Purpurascens', which has purple-green stems and fronds, and markedly pink-brown young shoots; the crested royal fern, 'Cristata', and 'Undulata' are smaller and have attractively tasselled foliage.

The interrupted fern, O. claytoniana, derives its common name from the spores that are borne around the stalk in a part of the frond which is devoid of leaflets. Leaflets above and below this spore area develop quite normally, giving the entire frond the appearance of having been interrupted.

Much smaller yet just as invasive is the plant variously known as the ostrich plume or shuttlecock fern (Matteuccia struthiopteris). It has a reputation for being a bit of a thug, as it will grow and multiply if it is happy with its soil and growing

environment. However, if you have the space it is a 'must'. It's deciduous, but come spring the new fronds unfurl in gold and bronze tints before becoming the freshest of lime greens.

The sensitive fern (Onoclea sensibilis) is a lovely fern reaching about 60cm (2ft) high. The triangular fronds have a pinkish tinge when they first open. Sadly, however, these fronds are most sensitive – hence its common name – to autumn frosts. Although the plant is as hardy as anything, the fronds are not. Even so, I wouldn't be without this plant.

Facts & Figures 40

Orchid growers over the past 200 years or so mostly associated osmunda ferns as the origins of the fibre compost in which their orchids were potted. Thankfully bark-based composts have now taken over as the number one medium for orchids, and the royal ferns are not tampered with anywhere near as much.

RIGHT: *The giant prickly rhubarb is the grandest of bog garden plants*

● Giant prickly rhubarb (*Gunnera manicata*)

It is almost compulsory for those of us with big water gardens to grow gunnera. It is our largest hardy herbaceous plant, and many call it the giant, or prickly rhubarb, because of the supposed similarity of its leaves; in truth the two plants are not even related. Close inspection will show that the plants are very different and, anyway, the gunnera is much more spectacular. As long as there is sufficient space, even in a small garden, gunnera will help to create an exotic atmosphere. The oversized leaves of gunnera afford shelter for all manner of garden wildlife – even waterfowl. Excellent plant combinations can be achieved with gunnera and ornamental grasses such as miscanthus.

FLOWERS *Conical clusters of small greenish-red flowers appear in late spring and early summer. These flower spikes can themselves reach 1.5m (5ft) in height. Rust-brown seed pods follow.*

A close-up of the complex flower spike of Gunnera manicata

LEAVES *The vast jagged and indented leaves are the main reason for growing gunnera. Individual leaves on some mature plants can reach to 2m (6ft) in diameter. These are carried on thick stems with nasty spikes on the biggest.*

CULTIVATION *Choose a position in full sun or medium shade, at the edge of larger ponds. Plant during spring. They are undemanding plants, as long as they have some shelter from the coldest of*

winds and the latest of frosts. Cut back the dry leaves in autumn, and in colder areas it is advisable to give the plants a protective mulch with straw, sacking or horticultural fleece. Gunnera tolerate most soils, but prefer deep, fertile soils with high moisture content. Feed with a general fertiliser in spring.

HARDINESS *Fairly hardy, tolerating temperatures down to -15˚C (5˚F).*

PROPAGATION *By division of larger clumps in spring, or by seeds sown fresh in the autumn. Choose a loam-based compost and store the growing seed in a sheltered cold frame.*

ORIGINS *South America, specifically the lower slopes of the Andes.*

HEIGHT *Up to 3m (10ft) when four years old.*

SPREAD *Up to 5m (16ft) when four years old.*

ALTERNATIVE PLANTS *The giant Chilean rhubarb*

Some leaves of gunnera can reach 2m (6ft) in diameter

(Gunnera tinctoria*) is slightly smaller and slightly hardier. Leaves on mature plants are just 1m (3ft) wide, and the overall height is 2m (6ft). Alternatively, opt for the dwarf, carpet-creeping gunnera, G. magellanica. It has bright green 'crinkled' leaves, and plants barely reach 10cm (4in) in height, with a spread of just 1m (3ft).*

● Globe flower (*Trollius europaeus*)

The globe flower has been attacked heavily by plant breeders over the years, and now there are many varieties which, in some respects, lack some of the charm of the original plant. It is a non-invasive hardy herbaceous perennial which looks most effective when grown in groups – as indeed it would be in the wild.

FLOWERS *Bright yellow spherical flowers are carried on wiry stems during late spring and early summer.*

LEAVES *Fern-like leaves, heavily divided and deep green.*

CULTIVATION *This plant likes a position in full sun or light shade, and looks good when growing amongst rocks. Plant in spring or autumn, preferably in groups. Mulch with well-rotted compost in the spring. During the flowering season, make sure you remove the faded flowers as quickly as possible, as this encourages more bloom to come.*

HARDINESS *Will survive temperatures as low as -20˚C.*

PROPAGATION *Divide plants in spring or autumn (overgrown clumps will need dividing every three or four years anyway). Alternatively, sow seeds under glass in spring.*

ORIGINS *Europe*

HEIGHT *Up to 75cm (30in).*

Trollius chinensis *'Golden Queen'*

The elegant leaves and flowers of goat's beard (Aruncus dioicus) *need plenty of room in which to grow*

SPREAD *Up to 45cm (18in).*

ALTERNATIVE PLANTS *More fiery colours than the yellow species are available from the numerous hybrids. Try the following:* Trollius *x* cultorum *'Alabaster', cream; 'Canary Bird', orange; 'Feuertroll' (also seen as 'Fireglobe'), deep orange;* Trollius chinensis *'Golden Queen', orange-yellow.*

● Goat's beard (*Aruncus dioicus*)

The elegant leaves, majestic flowers and tall stems make this plant an erect and stately star of the bog garden. The normal species needs plenty of room in which to spread, so if space is not a problem, this plant is a must.

FLOWERS *In early and mid-summer, tiny, cream-white blooms appear on large fluffy flowerheads. Arguably, aruncus is just as attractive in the early flower stage – when the stems are delicately lined with tiny round buds – as it is when the great creamy plumes have all exploded into foaming flowers.*

LEAVES *Numerous deeply serrated leaflets of fresh green are arranged on long stems.*

CULTIVATION *Plant during the spring or autumn, directly into rich, moist and peaty soil. Aruncus prefers a position in light or moderate shade. There is little maintenance required: like other perennials, cut back the dead top-growth in late autumn, and take this opportunity for a general tidy-up. Mulch soil-grown plants with compost in the spring or autumn. Provide a few handfuls of general fertilizer in the spring. Aruncus has very stiff stems, so does not need*

Facts & Figures 41

The feathery flowerheads of goat's beard (*Aruncus dioicus*) are really most unexpected for something that belongs to the same plant family as the rose.

staking. Clumps can grow large, so should be divided every three or four years. Aruncus is virtually pest and disease free.

HARDINESS *Very hardy, tolerating temperatures down to -20°C.*

PROPAGATION *Divide the spreading roots of larger clumps in spring or autumn. Or sow seeds in summer or early autumn in a humus-rich, soil-based compost. Provide protection, such as that supplied by a cold frame or unheated greenhouse.*

ORIGINS *The mountain woods and shady stream-sides of central Europe, China, Japan and North America.*

HEIGHT *Up to 2m (6ft).*

SPREAD *Up to 1.2m (4ft).*

ALTERNATIVE PLANTS *The old name for this plant is* Aruncus sylvester, *and some nurseries may still be selling it under this name. The normal species is the best, but for smaller gardens there is the variety 'Kneiffii', which grows to about half the size. The leaves of this smaller form look as though they have been eaten to the veins by some creature, but this makes them very attractively lacy.*

● Grasses as ornamental features

Only a few years ago, no more than a handful of decorative, ornamental grasses would have been listed in plant catalogues. Now they are very fashionable, and there is a bewildering array of species and varieties, from the architectural pampas grass to the clump-forming smaller forms, like festuca. Not all grasses like a really wet or waterlogged soil – moist but free-draining seems to be the motto.

CULTIVATION *Plant in spring, in full sun or light shade. Mulch in autumn and spring and give a balanced general fertilizer in spring. Leave the top-growth over winter, and reduce it in early spring before new*

Schoenoplectus lacustris *'Albescens'*

growth commences. Keep the clumps healthy by dividing every four or five years.

HARDINESS *Varies depending on the species, but most will survive temperatures as low as -15°C, some even lower.*

PROPAGATION *By division in autumn or spring.*

RECOMMENDED SPECIES *One grass which revels in boggy conditions is the reed sweet grass (*Glyceria maxima var. variegata*), which is vigorous and can be invasive – growing in a sunken container will alleviate this problem. Its young foliage has a pinkish hue which becomes boldly variegated with white and yellow as it ages.*

*The cream variegated grasses are particularly attractive. One which never fails to impress is the golden hakone grass (*Hakonechloa macra *'Alboaurea') with its brilliant yellow-striped blades. It is a low grower, not exceeding 30cm (12in), and forms a dense mat which in time becomes a sizeable clump.*

*One of the brightest of grasses is the golden wood millet (*Milium effusum *'Aureum'). It is at its most*

Facts & Figures 42

How do you tell the difference between true grasses, sedges and rushes? The following rule doesn't apply in every case, but it will be a general guide: take a leaf from one of these groups and look at it in cross section. A true grass will be fairly flat or 'V'-shaped, a sedge leaf will be triangular, whilst a rush will be circular.

Carex elata 'Aurea' may also be found under the name 'Bowles' Golden'

spectacular in spring when the growths are young. It has a loose-growing, tufted habit, and will not get taller than 60cm (2ft). It can also self-seed, but it will not become a nuisance.

Another fabulous variety is Bowles' Golden sedge (Carex elata 'Aurea'). Its brown, fairly uninspiring flowers appear in mid-spring. But after these have faded, the plant throws up long, arching leaves of the strongest yellow. A very narrow green margin is present on each leaf making the plant most spectacular. The colour deepens until mid-summer, when it fades gradually to green.

A rush with grass-like properties, Schoenoplectus lacustris, is seen in many natural and cultivated gardens, but is often disregarded because it appears 'normal', with no apparent outstanding qualities. However, on closer inspection, its foliage is variegated and in its own way quite striking. Look for the

varieties 'Albescens' with longitudinal green and white stripes, or 'Zebrinus' with horizontal cream stripes on a background of green.

The pennisetums are grasses best grown in a sunny position, otherwise they will need some protection. One of the best clump-formers is Pennisetum orientale with light green, rather hairy leaves. It is grown mainly for its flower spikes rising 45cm (18in) high, which are of a bottle-brush shape, mauve-grey initially, slowly changing to a golden brown.

The festucas are generally low-growing, ideal subjects for the front of a border. They require light, well-drained soil, and for best effect should be planted into small groups. 'Golden Toupee' forms a neat, tight cushion with fine, almost needle-like leaves which, like the milium, is best in spring when it is an almost iridescent yellow. As it ages, the colour turns to lime green. Among the most popular festucas

Iris sibirica *'Perry's Blue'*

Iris ensata *'Barr Purple East'*

Iris sibirica *'Silver Edge'*

Iris ensata *'Flying Tiger'*

are those with blue-grey leaves, such as the excellent *'Elijah Blue'*.

Meadow foxtail grass (Alopecurus pratensis *'Aureovariegatus'*) is worth growing in a sunny spot, but don't be misled by the common name: it makes a fabulous plant for the bog garden. In early summer it produces the most delightful, soft, tubular flower head with a slight purple hue. The leaves have some of the most golden stripes of any grass.

Lastly, if you want something with a hot colour, choose the Japanese blood grass (Imperata cylindrica *'Rubra'*). Its young leaves are as red as you can get.

● Irises

Several species of iris will flourish in the damp soil of a bog garden, but only two are really popular and neither of them likes over-wet soil in winter.

Iris ensata (which used to be known, and is still sometimes sold as, *I. kaempferi*) is the delightful Japanese clematis iris, so-called because the blooms flatten out to resemble the star-shaped blooms of clematis. It grows to a height of between 60–75cm (24–30in), and flowers during late spring and early summer. The downside is that an acid soil is essential. The leaves are broad and the flowers are large and flattened. *I. ensata* can be grown from seed; there may be some variation of colour, but all should be good.

There are, literally, hundreds of varieties of

Iris ensata *var.* spontanea *produces deep purple flowers, each with a fetching gold streak*

ensata. Three of the best are 'Flying Tiger' (pale blue with yellow inside the petals), 'Barr Purple East' (deep purple), and *I. ensata* var. *spontanea* (purple with a golden streak inside the petals).

Meanwhile, the Siberian iris, *I. sibirica*, is an easier plant to grow. I have two clumps of 'Perry's Blue', untouched for about nine years, and they're growing on quite a limy soil. They could probably do with a bit of thinning once the flowers have finished; the centres of ageing clumps tend to become 'bald' with a ring of growth progressively moving outwards each year.

At flowering time the first of two buds from each stem opens and does its thing. The second bud opens as the first fades. At the end of the flowering season the highly glossy green seed pods are formed, and these have an attraction all of their own; remove them in the autumn to keep the clump tidy.

The leaves of *I. sibirica* are grass-like, and the flowers smaller than most other water irises, but there are many excellent varieties, and several good dwarf forms, including 'Flight of Butterflies' (dark blue veined purple), and 'Silver Edge' (deep blue with white edges to the petals).

If the ground remains very wet in winter, try growing *I. orientalis*, formerly known as *I. ochroleuca*. It is easy to grow, and even grows in salty marshes in its wild habitat in the Middle East. It usually grows to 1m (3ft), producing white and egg-yolk yellow flowers.

To propagate all of the irises mentioned here, specially if the desire is to keep the offspring true to their parent, dividing the clumps into individual plants after flowering is the only method. In most cases, the sooner this is done after the flowers fade, the better, but with *I. ensata* it is best to wait until autumn, before the leaves have finally died down.

● Lady's mantle (*Alchemilla mollis*)

This is one of the most familiar of border plants, beloved of flower arrangers for the soft, wispy green flowers and thick, uniquely serrated leaves. For the gardener it is a fine, architectural hardy herbaceous perennial, and it is a must for any bog garden. Although there are around 30 species of alchemilla, this is the form that is best for the bog garden.

FLOWERS *Tiny, soft yellow-green flowers are held in umbrella-like clusters throughout summer.*

Lady's mantle (Alchemilla mollis) *is used often by flower arrangers*

LEAVES *Large, many-lobed leaves with fine serrations appear to be both waxy and downy at the same time. It's a cliché to eulogize over the apparent compulsion for droplets of rainwater and dew to collect in the bowls of the leaves, but they do make this plant a little special.*

CULTIVATION *Ideally, this plant needs dappled shade, as direct sunlight for long periods during summer days can turn some of the leaves crispy. Mulch around the base of the plant in spring and/or autumn, and it is advisable to throw a handful of general fertilizer around the base of the plant in spring. Remove the faded flowerheads and cut all old growth down to ground level at the end of autumn.*

HARDINESS *Extremely hardy, tolerating temperatures down to -20°C, and probably even lower.*

PROPAGATION *By division in spring or autumn. Or by seed sown in autumn. This plant will readily self-sow and come up in some unusual places in the garden; it is not, however, usually regarded as a nuisance, as the young seedlings can be most welcome.*

ORIGINS *This has a fairly widespread origin, from Europe, to Asia, Labrador and even Greenland.*

HEIGHT *Up to 50cm (20in).*

SPREAD *Up to 50cm (20in).*

● Marsh gentian (*Gentiana pneumonanthe*)

No other bog garden plant will provide as intense a blue as this unusual but very choice wild flower. For this plant to thrive and achieve its full impact, the soil needs to be damp and rich in organic matter and, perhaps most important of all, acid.

FLOWERS *Clusters of rich, deep blue trumpet-shaped flowers appear at the ends of stems during mid- to late summer.*

LEAVES *Lush green, shiny and lance-shaped on short, slender stems.*

CULTIVATION *In spring plant in full sun, or light to moderate shade. Mulch with garden compost after planting, and annually each spring. Feed with a general fertilizer at the same time. If the leaves turn yellow in summer, the soil is not acid enough, so water it with sequestered iron to restore the pH levels. This gentian resents disturbance, so leave it well alone once it's established.*

HARDINESS *It will survive temperatures down to -20°C.*

PROPAGATION *Take softwood cuttings in summer, rooting them in a propagator with slight bottom*

With its rhubarb-like leaves, Rheum palmatum *makes an exotic addition to the bog garden*

heat. Seeds can be sown in early spring, again in a propagator, at kept at around 20°C.

ORIGINS *Native throughout the northern hemisphere.*

HEIGHT *Up to 30cm (12in).*

SPREAD *Up to 25cm (10in).*

ALTERNATIVE PLANTS *The willow gentian (*Gentiana asclepiadea*) produces typical gentian-blue flowers on stems up to 60cm (24in) high, and tolerates some lime in the soil; it also has a white form, 'Alba', and various pink or pale blue varieties.*

● Ornamental rhubarb (*Rheum palmatum*)

Unlike gunnera (see page 106), which 'pretends' to be an ornamental rhubarb plant, this really is one. Although much smaller than gunnera it is, in its own, way just as dramatic and its leaves combined with the elongated flowerheads make

this quite an exotic addition to the bog garden.

FLOWERS *During late spring and early summer small, red or purple flowers appear in large plumes on rigid purplish stalks. The stalks can rise to a height of 3m (10ft).*

LEAVES *The leaves are deeply lobed, and are of a rich green or purple (with a reddish tinge to the undersides). Each leaf can be 90cm (3ft) across when mature.*

CULTIVATION *Plant in full sun or part-shade, but make sure the soil is moist and rich. Feed with a general fertiliser in spring. Cut down all faded flowerheads in late autumn, and cover the dormant crowns with straw or horticultural fleece.*

HARDINESS *Will survive temperatures down to around -15°C.*

PROPAGATION *Divide crowns in spring; plants will need dividing every four or five years.*

ORIGINS *China.*

HEIGHT *Mature plants can grow up to 2m (6ft) – not including the height of the flower head.*

SPREAD *Up to 2m (7ft).*

ALTERNATIVE PLANTS Rheum palmatum rubrum *produces rich, pink flower spikes; 'Atrosanguineum' has red spring leaves, and red flowers in summer; 'Bowles' Crimson' is a deeper red and 'Ace of Hearts' is a miniature version with pink flowers and leaves that are rich red beneath.*

● Plantain lilies (*Hosta* spp.)

With more than 70 species and hundreds of modern varieties (which are being added to every year), there are few hardy herbaceous plants that can match the variety, diversity of form, texture and leaf colourings of the hosta. The Chinese *Hosta plantaginea* was the first hosta introduced to European gardens, in the late 1700s, and others quickly followed, mainly from Japan. Hostas are, of course, principally grown for their large, graceful leaves. In summer they produce long stems of small, nodding, lily-like flowers in shades of lilac, mauve and purple, as well as a few which are pure white. Some are fragrant.

The leaves vary in size from those just a few centimetres long, to the largest which are dinner plate-sized. Just as the sizes vary, so too do the textures of the leaves, from very smooth, through to shiny, dull, matt and even corrugated. Add to these variables the bewildering array of leaf colours and variegations and one can see why they are among some of our most popular plants.

CULTIVATION *Plant in spring, in a position that receives full sun, or dappled shade. Mulch in spring or*

Hosta undulata *var.* albomarginata

Hosta fortunei *var.* albopicta

autumn, and give a handful of general fertilizer per plant in spring. Cut back dead flower stalks as soon as they have faded, and cut or pull away tattered foliage as soon as it starts to look bad. The biggest problem, and famously so, is the attacking of hosta leaves by slugs and snails.

HARDINESS *Fully hardy, surviving temperatures down to around -20°C.*

PROPAGATION *By division in autumn or spring.*

RECOMMENDED SPECIES *Probably the most popular species of hosta is* H. fortunei, *and one of the most attractive forms is* H. fortunei *var.* albopicta. *It has bright yellow leaves distinctively edged with green in spring, which change to all-over green as they age. Meanwhile,* H. fortunei *var.* Aureomarginata *has leaves of a rich dark green with a yellow border, and* H. fortunei *var.* hyacintha *has slightly shiny, small green leaves with long points.*

Hosta crispula is a great favourite, with striking white-margined broad, pointed dark green leaves. It also offers stems of lilac-purple flowers in mid-summer. H. decorata *has bold-ribbed leaves with cream margins; the flowers are pale purple.* H. elata *is among the earliest to flower, with pale lilac blooms in early summer, held aloft pale green, matt leaves with wavy edges.*

Wavy edged foliage is a characteristic of the varieties of Hosta undulata. *One of the earliest varieties is* H. undulata *var.* albomarginata *(also seen sometimes named 'Thomas Hogg'); it has a strong creamy-white edge to the leaves.*

Primula japonica *produces flowers in several 'candelabra' tiers*

Primulas

Whichever bog plants you grow, there should always be room for a primula or ten. The primula genus ranks as one of the largest, most variable, durable and likeable of all plant genera. There are primulas for growing in pots, on rockeries, in flower beds, in woodland dells and at the sides of a pond.

CULTIVATION *Sunny or lightly shaded places are best, and primulas prefer a fairly rich, organic, slightly acid soil. Mulch lightly around the plants in spring. Cut back dead flower heads and foliage where feasible, and divide the plants every three or four years. Depending on your chosen primulas, you may find that they are susceptible to such garden pests as slugs and snails, viruses, fungal leaf spots and burrowing leaf miner grubs.*

HARDINESS *Fully hardy, surviving temperatures down to around -20°C.*

PROPAGATION *Sow fresh seeds on to the surface of soil-based potting composts under glass in spring. Germination is slow, can be erratic, and some hybrids and strains will not come true from seed (that is, the offspring will not always be identical to the parents). Alternatively, divide mature plants in spring or autumn.*

Primula pulverulenta *is a candelabra species with flowers from pale pink to mauve*

The orchid primula (P. vialii)

RECOMMENDED SPECIES *Some primulas are temperamental, or elusive, but the following small selection is sure to provide colour and interest if you give them the preferred growing conditions as outlined above.*

Primula aurantiaca is one of the so-called candelabra primulas (meaning that, like others, it bears its flowers in rounded clusters, or whorls, at intervals along the main central stem). It has striking orange or orange-red blooms in late spring and early summer, which is slightly earlier than the other candelabras. The flower stems can reach 75cm (30in) in height.

Primula japonica is possibly the best-known candelabra primula, with lush leaves and several tiers of red, pink or white flowers opening at stages throughout early and mid-summer. Four of the best varieties are: 'Alba', white; 'Apple Blossom', pink; 'Miller's Crimson', deep pink; and 'Postford White', white.

Other candelabras include Primula beesiana, *deep red with yellow centres;* P. × bulleesiana, *featuring a wide range of colours from yellow, orange and pink through to red and purple, and* P. pulverulenta, *pale pink or mauve.*

The drumstick primula, P. denticulata, *is extremely popular, with its neat globular pink-purple heads 8cm (3in) across. There are many garden forms, the flower colours of which are generally given away by their varietal names: 'Glenroy Crimson', 'Inshriach Carmine', 'Prichard's Ruby', 'Robinson's Red' and 'Snowball'.*

The Himalayan cowslip (Primula florindae) is similar to a tall wild cowslip

The orchid primula, P. vialii, *is one of the most stunning of all primula species. It is distinct from the others in that it has startling spikes of bright red buds, and in the early part of the summer the lowest buds open to mauve or lilac blooms. The top buds are the last to open, giving the whole flower head a dual red/lilac combination.*

There is little that can beat a patch of Himalayan cowslips, P. florindae. *This plant resembles a very tall, shaggy cowslip – at around 80cm (32in) on mature specimens – with slightly powdery sulphur yellow flower heads in early summer. A smaller version of the Himalayan cowslip is* P. sikkimensis, *which has its origins in the Chinese marshlands. It has bright yellow flowers in mid-spring.*

● Rodgersia (*Rodgersia aesculifolia*)

This is one of those plants that looks perfect next to a woodland stream or large pond, but incongruous when grown anywhere else in the garden. Its leaves look as if they should be growing high up on a horse chestnut tree (aesculus), but this plant is, of course, a border plant. Lovers of bold, dramatic, architectural plants will adore this.

The flowers and leaves of Rodgersia aesculifolia

The dramatic – and rather exotic – skunk cabbage (Lysichiton americanus)

FLOWERS *In mid-summer, plumes of many tiny pinkish-red blossoms are held well above the foliage.*

LEAVES *Large, shining and rich green, usually evenly suffused reddish bronze. Each palmate leaf has an impressive network of veins.*

CULTIVATION *This needs a moist soil if it is to do well. Mulch in the spring and autumn and give a handful of general fertilizer in the spring. Leave the flower heads in place once they are finished as the reddish seed heads come along much later in the season. Do not disturb the plants once they are established.*

HARDINESS *Will survive temperatures down to around -15°C.*

PROPAGATION *Spring divisions of the tough surface rhizomes will soon develop into their own clumps.*

ORIGINS *China.*

HEIGHT *Up to 1.5m (5ft).*

SPREAD *Up to 1m (3ft).*

ALTERNATIVE PLANTS Rodgersia pinnata *'Superba' has deeply divided leaves and white flowers;* R. podophylla *has palm-shaped leaves and cream flowers; and* R. sambucifolia *has leaves like an elder, and white flowers.*

● Skunk cabbage (*Lysichiton americanus*)

What an unpleasant name for a wonderful plant. When sniffed at close quarters, the heavy aroma produced by the foliage will explain why it is so called. This really is a star of the bog garden, however: its eye-catching golden yellow spathe flowers appear before the large, spectacular leaves. It really pays to grow this next to water, where the reflection can add to the magnificence. You can tell I'm a fan.

FLOWERS *Large, bright yellow spathes in typical arum style; each one can be 30cm (12in) in length.*

LEAVES *The leaves are long, rounded a fresh yellow-green. They emerge in summer after the flowers have faded.*

CULTIVATION *Plant in spring, 75cm (30in) apart if growing more than one. The soil should be enriched with plenty of organic matter, for these are very hungry plants. The best position is in partial shade, although it likes growing in full sun almost as much. This is a relatively undemanding plant, but it would pay to provide a twice yearly mulch in spring and*

*The oriental bog arum (*Lysichiton camschatcensis*) produces white spathes*

autumn. Feed with a general fertilizer in spring. Do not disturb the plants once they are established.

HARDINESS *Will survive temperatures down to around -15˚C.*

PROPAGATION *In late spring or early summer sow fresh seed in moist soil. Self-sown seedlings – which can get out of hand – can be transplanted at any time.*

ORIGINS *The western side of North America.*

HEIGHT *Up to 1m (3ft).*

SPREAD *Up to 60cm (2ft).*

ALTERNATIVE PLANTS *This plant is also referred to as the American bog arum, and the botanical name is often spelt wrongly, i.e.* Lysichitum americanum. *The oriental bog arum (*L. camschatcensis*) is a slightly smaller plant, with white spathes.*

● Water avens (*Geum rivale*)

This is a hardy woodland plant which enjoys a wetter soil than many of its compatriots. It also exists in many cultivated forms with a wide selection of flower colours. It is closely related to the garden geums, but its flowers are much more dainty.

FLOWERS *During late spring and early summer small pinkish-purple bells hang in loose heads on arching, hairy stalks.*

LEAVES *Small, rich green, rounded and slightly toothed at the edges.*

CULTIVATION *Plant in spring or autumn in a lightly shaded spot. If planting more than one, set them out 30cm (12in) apart. These plants do not require staking. Mulch in the autumn with moist, well-rotted garden compost. Cut down top-growth in late autumn.*

HARDINESS *Will survive temperatures down to around -20˚C.*

PROPAGATION *Divide the plants in autumn or spring (they will need this every third or fourth year anyway).*

ORIGINS *Throughout the northern hemisphere.*

HEIGHT *Up to 45cm (18in).*

SPREAD *Up to 45cm (18in).*

ALTERNATIVE PLANTS *Among the selected forms are 'Album' with white flowers; 'Leonard's Variety', pinkish-orange flowers; and 'Variegatum', with cream marks on the leaves.*

FISH AND WILDLIFE

CHAPTER 9

HARDY POND FISH

Much of the enjoyment derived from a pond is as a result of the fish that swim around in it. In fact I feel that a pond is not complete if it doesn't have some fish, which add colour and animation to the scene, particularly in formal pools. A side benefit is that they can reduce significantly the number of midges and mosquitoes that frequent your garden. It is, however, important to understand that fish can vary greatly in their requirements, so much so that a pond which is perfect for one species, may be a deathtrap for another. For this reason I am going to explain which fish do what, and how to make your pond the best environment for them.

BUYING POND FISH

Once you have built your pond and filled it with tap-water, the urge to put some fish in it can be enormous. Don't. A new pond must settle down – six weeks is not an unrealistic time to wait – before introducing fish. During the first couple of weeks the fresh water in the pond will turn a browny-green colour, and become progressively cloudier as micro-organisms multiply. A variety of plants should be in place, including plenty of submerged oxygenators. These will help to absorb dissolved minerals, and of course provide oxygen to the water. The fish will be afforded some protection by these, and will also use them for green food. Floating and deep water plants provide the shade which is very welcome on hot summer days. By the sixth week the water should be clear.

It is worth remembering that most fish scavenge. They'll nose around and disturb freshly planted aquatics, so it is important to allow the plants time to establish before the fish are introduced, and to cover the soil in the pots with a thick layer of gravel, otherwise the soil will be displaced, and the water will turn brown.

Buying some fish from a garden centre, transporting them home, and then putting them in the pond, with no forethought about the environment they were in, and the one to which you are now subjecting them, can result in a high, if not total, mortality rate. So, to start with, it is essential to know just how many fish, and of what size, your pond can accommodate safely. Work this out before you start spending money

Fish make great – and comparatively undemanding – pets for children

on buying the fish, (see Facts & Figures Tip 43 below). Of course, you may exceed the recommended quantity of fish under certain conditions if, for instance, you have a pond that is very deep, or you have installed an over-sized filtration system, but this is unlikely for a beginner to the hobby.

The best time to stock a new pond, or add further fish to an existing complement, is in late spring or early summer when temperatures are fairly stable but, when buying fish you do take a bit of a gamble. No one can say with 100% conviction whether a fish is absolutely free of disease or parasites, regardless of how healthy it may look. This six-point plan for detecting signs of a healthy fish should serve as a useful guide:

1. LOOK FOR A LIVELY DISPOSITION. *Fish such as goldfish, orfe and koi should be constantly on the move, and even dart about when 'spooked'. If they seem lethargic, or float on the surface, or lie relatively still at the bottom, then they are best avoided. However, note that bottom-dwellers, like tench, should be at the bottom and they move quite slowly – this is normal.*

2. CHECK THE FINS. *A healthy fish should have its fins well extended. The fin on the back (the dorsal) regularly extends and collapses as the fish hovers or changes direction; it is usually collapsed as the fish moves its tail fin (the caudal) to propel itself forward. Any damaged fins will indicate that the fish has been in a scrap, and it should be avoided.*

3. LOOK AT THE BODY. *Damaged or missing scales are unsightly, but not necessarily a sign of ill health. Scales can usually regenerate without subsequent infection. However, if there any blood spots, or fungal growth (looking like cotton wool), then do not buy it – or other fish from the same tank.*

4. EXAMINE THE EYES. *A healthy fish should have clear eyes. If they are 'milky' in appearance, it is a possible sign that the fish is injured or otherwise unhealthy. This can be difficult if the fish you want is moving about quickly, or hugging the bottom of the tank, but it is worth taking the time to find out.*

5. CHECK THE COLOURS. *The scales of a fish are covered by a protective layer of mucus, which tends to enhance the colour of the fish and make the body bright, vivid and clear. If the fish is unhealthy, there can be a check to the mucus, or an excess in the production of mucus, both of which can cause the appearance to be dull or cloudy.*

When introducing new fish, place the bag in the pond water for about ten minutes

6. OBSERVE THE SWIMMING TECHNIQUE. *A regular pace, in straight lines, and in a considered way. This is how a healthy fish should swim. It should not roll about, or lose its balance, or keep floating upwards, or sinking downwards. The one word of caution here is if a fish is eating, or has just had a meal, it can sometimes sway as it chews.*

INTRODUCING FISH

Fish make great pets for children, but are highly sensitive to changes in temperature and water quality, so avoid any shocks when transferring them to the pond. When you buy fish from a pet shop or aquatic centre they will be swimming around in a plastic bag. After a trip in the car (and particularly if the fish were previously housed in an indoor aquarium), the water will be warm, or at least the equivalent of 'room

Facts & Figures 43

When deciding how many fish can safely be introduced to your pond, follow this equation: allow 155cm² (24 sq in) of water surface area per 2.5cm (1in) length of fish – excluding tails! Once the calculation has been made, reduce it by 25%, to allow for the fish to grow.

Gradually allow some of the pond water into the bag

temperature'. So, for best results, follow this simple process:

1. *Place the bag containing the fish in the pond, and leave it for ten minutes so that the water temperature inside the bag reduces to the same as the pond water.*

2. *Introduce a little pond water into the bag. Leave for ten minutes.*

3. *Add a little more water and leave for a further ten minutes.*

4. *Push the bag on to its side so that the fish can swim away freely.*

   Remember at all times that fish are living creatures, and if you treat them right they will reward you with life, vitality, colour and even friendliness. Get a routine in your feeding and as long as you don't frighten them, they'll start to trust you and come up to you.

Facts & Figures 44

When fish are prone to disease, sudden death and red fins, this is a sure sign that the water has a high level of acidity (or low pH). Other indications are when oxygenating plants do not multiply well; biological pond filters do not work properly, and water snails develop thin, pitted shells.

ABOVE: *Common goldfish*

ABOVE: *Bristol shubunkin*

Ranchu

ABOVE: *Comet*

Black moor

SPECIES TO CHOOSE

There are in excess of 20,000 species of fish in nature, and most of these are marine-based. A small number are freshwater fish, and only a tiny number of these are suitable for keeping in ponds. Nevertheless, of the few species available to us, there is a huge range of hybrids, shapes, colours, habits and sizes. And the good news is that every few years a new type of fish, or strain of fish, becomes available to the pond-keeper.

The common goldfish

It is said that the common goldfish is the best known fish in the world and we can all instantly recognize it. It is fairly long-lived fish – 15 years is not unusual – and millions are bred annually

Facts & Figures 45

There is documentary evidence that goldfish were kept as pets as long ago as the Chinese Sung dynasty (960–1279).

ABOVE: *Veiltail*

by fish farms, which also makes them quite cheap to buy.

Originally from China and parts of Siberia, the goldfish is a hardy breed, able to withstand a range of temperatures from above 30°C down to practically freezing. As a child I well remember the cold British winter of 1963. We had about eight goldfish in a large metal water tank in the greenhouse. The water froze solid, even under glass, all bar about three inches at the bottom. They were probably iced up for three or four days in total but, by speedily defrosting the ice, we managed to save most of the fish.

Facts & Figures 46

When fish are prone to fungal diseases and gill disorders, this is a sure sign that the water has a high level of alkalinity (or high pH). Other indications are when oxygenating plants are covered in a slimy coating; water plants display a yellowing of the leaves when in full growth, and the water smells slightly of ammonia.

The golden tench scavenges in the mud at the bottom of the pond

Goldfish can grow up to about 30cm (12in) from head to tail, if the conditions are right and the pool large enough. Fancy varieties are usually considerably smaller. The 'normal' goldfish is short-finned, usually orange but also in other single colour variations (although curiously not in the olive green that is the natural colour of its ancestors). Centuries of selective breeding have produced over 100 'official' varieties of goldfish.

Facts & Figures 47

Goldfish are mainly orange, so why do we call them 'gold'? This actually refers to the shiny gold colour of the wild type fish, as well as in the juvenile stages of many cultivated species.

Here are some of the most commonly seen:

BRISTOL SHUBUNKIN. *Shubunkins are fancy versions of the goldfish with larger fins and generally with more graceful, ornamental qualities. The Bristol is single-tailed, long-finned and has mottled coloration which normally includes a little blue.*

COMET. *These are sleeker cousins of the shubunkin, with a longer tail, preferably pointed.*

MOOR. *Double-tailed black fish, sometimes with protruding eyes, rather more tender than the others. Today there are varieties with chocolate, and chocolate and orange colourings.*

RANCHU. *Oval-bodied, with a curved back profile minus the dorsal fin. Usually orange.*

VEILTAIL. *Oval-bodied double-tailed with long, flowing fins.*

FANCIES: *Fantails and Orandas are tender and are really at their best in a coldwater aquarium. However, they make good pond inhabitants for the warmer months.*

BREEDING: most goldfish possess the same habits, i.e. they eat their own eggs! The mature females scatter the eggs amongst water plants, usually when the temperature rises above 20°C – conditions can certainly be favourable in late spring, particularly in shallow waters.

Golden orfe

These, also known as the 'ide' fish, are perfect for larger ponds – with a minimum surface area of 4m² (43 sq ft). In the wild the orfe is silver, but the golden form has been bred for use in garden ponds, along with blue and marbled variants. They are native to various parts of Northern Europe, particularly the River Danube. They are fast movers, staying near the surface of the water – a very obliging form of behaviour as far as humans are concerned.

Orfe are usually sold as specimens of 8–10cm (3–4in) long, but in time they will reach 45cm (18in) if conditions are right. They need to swim in water that is oxygen-rich and for this reason they seem to enjoy the splashes from fountains and waterfalls. They can suffer when the oxygen runs low, for instance during dull, thundery weather.

BREEDING: in late spring the female scatters her eggs among fine-leaved water plants. Hatching takes place in around 20 days.

Golden tench

This fish, which in the wild inhabits the still waters of rivers, large ponds and even sand pits, can grow to a massive 71cm (28in), although 30–41cm (12–16in) is more usual for a healthy adult in a large domestic pond. Tench are excellent scavengers and feed off the muddy bottoms of the pond. Although they are very hardy fish, during particularly cold weather they will bury themselves in the mud for some protection.

Golden rudd feeds on worms, insects and vegetation, and associates well with other fish

Grass carp can grow to over 1m (3ft) in length

The original, if you like 'wild' form, was the green tench but for garden pond situations the cultivated golden tench is better, as it is more decorative and more easily seen.

Tench are undemanding, being able to survive in relatively acidic water (low pH), with fairly low oxygen levels. The natural food of the tench comprises various insects, worms and young shoots of water vegetation.

BREEDING: a mature female can lay up to 900,000 adhesive eggs among aquatic plants and weed in late spring and early summer. Hatching can take between six to eight days.

Golden rudd

The body of this fish is actually silver, but with a golden hue. Its scales are large and rough-looking, and make identification fairly easy. In a pond situation the rudd can grow to 41cm (16in) in length, feeding on worms, insects and certain aquatic vegetation. It is found wild in slow-running rivers in most parts of Europe north of the Pyrenees.

The rudd inhabits the surface and midwater section of the pond, and associates well with other fish, particularly orfe.

BREEDING: a large female rudd can lay as many as 200,000 adhesive eggs during spring and early summer. Hatching takes between 8 to 15 days, depending on the temperature.

Grass carp

This species can grow to over 1m (3ft) in length so a large pond is required. Although it is a fine fish, with certain excellent qualities, I hesitate to recommend it, a) because it consumes large amounts of most water plants, with relish, and b) because the larger fish can also leap, so it is not unusual for them to jump out of the pond and perish. In its favour, most grass carp kept in ornamental pools are albinos, which are particularly attractive against dark-sided ponds, and they will actually consume quantities of unwanted vegetation, including duckweed and algae.

BREEDING: this fish needs a temperature of around

27–29°C to spawn, so is unlikely to breed in the confined ponds of temperate zone gardens (which, bearing in mind their eventual size, is quite possibly a relief to know).

FEEDING FISH

Providing clean water (which we have already discussed in Chapter 4) and supplying the correct, balanced food, are the two most important considerations we can give our fish. Feeding is a crucial, life-giving (or life-taking if it is done badly) part of the maintenance programme. Don't forget, also, that sheer pleasure can be had from seeing a clutch of champing mouths eagerly respond to our scatterings. Feeding fish is as much a bonding exercise as it is providing sustenance.

Fish are generally omnivorous, naturally eating both plant and animal material, some species scouring the bottom of the pond for worms, shrimps, algae and even decaying detritus. So, if fish can survive without help in the wild, do our pond fish actually need any supplementary food from us? If you possess a lush wildlife pond teeming with insects and crustaceans, and have only a few fish, then the answer would be 'no'. However, most pond set-ups mean that providing supplementary food is the safest option for maintaining a healthy stock of fish.

Do not be tempted to feed your fish at all if the temperature drops below 7°C (44°F). It is actually harmful to feed fish when it is so cold that their metabolic processes, including digestion, slow right down, increasing the danger of food rotting inside the gut. Between 7–14°C (44–57°F), easily digestible foods with high wheatgerm content can be introduced. When the water temperature stabilizes above 15°C (59°F), high protein, growth-inducing feed can be used; increase the

Facts & Figures 48

In Romania there is a population of rudd that has adapted to living in hot springs where the water temperature is regularly in the 28–34°C (82–93°F) range. It is said that the fish die if the water temperature drops below 20°C (68°F).

Facts & Figures 49

If you desire a true wildlife pond, then keeping fish may not be such a good idea. Apart from predations by cats and herons, the fish are at the top of the food chain in a pond, and will readily devour tadpoles, dragonfly larvae and many other desirable creatures.

frequency of meals to two or three times a day as the temperature rises.

Skim off any remaining food from the surface of your pond if it has been uneaten after ten minutes or so. Failing to do this will result in surplus food falling to the bottom to be fed on by bacteria, whose toxic by-products can poison fish.

The main types of pond fish food are manufactured flakes and pellets, frozen aquatic organisms and live food. When buying manufactured food, look out for types that float well, bringing the fish to the surface to feed. Choose a size of food that is appropriate to your fish.

Like us, fish need a balanced diet, so check the packet to ensure that the protein content – fishmeal, soya and egg mainly – is around 30% for summer foods. For spring and autumn feeding change to makes with higher carbohydrate (wheatgerm-based) levels. Vitamin C boosts fish immunity to disease, and is added to some higher quality foods.

Frozen food is well worth tracking down. It generally comes in all the same varieties as live food and can be stored in your freezer. Some brands are gamma irradiated prior to freezing to kill off the pathogenic parasites and bacteria that can cause fish diseases if introduced to your pond via live food.

If you wish to adopt an overall more organic approach to feeding your fish, it is possible to buy many of the organisms that fish would encounter in the wild. Earthworms, chopped lettuce, the occasional slice of orange (peel and all), are all nutritious additions. Even grass clippings are devoured by the grass carp, but make sure that no weedkillers or noxious chemicals were used on the lawn previously.

CHAPTER 10

INTRODUCTION TO KOI KEEPING

The fish with the best social mastery are the koi (real name nishikigoi). They will feed from your hand quite readily, and over a period of time they can be seen to develop characters of their own. But to keep even one koi successfully, you should provide relatively sophisticated filtration, water movement and oxygenation, year-round care, special food and, of course, regularly check and maintain high water quality. Keeping koi requires investment and dedication.

Although koi are descendants of the common carp their selective breeding over the years has

meant that they are much more particular about the water conditions in which they live. Maintenance of good water quality all year round is, therefore, of the utmost importance.

Great pleasure is gained from viewing koi swimming lazily in clear, clean water, watching them grow and their patterns change as they develop and age. It is, therefore, the general rule that a koi pond will not be planted. Some people do keep koi alongside other coldwater fish, quite successfully, in planted 'ornamental' ponds. Keeping large koi in these conditions can, however, present problems. Because koi are

Koi are voracious eaters and can tear plants to pieces .

voracious creatures that will tear plants to pieces, a planted pond is generally not feasible. Some parts of the plants will be eaten but others will sink to the bottom of the pond, whilst other pieces may be sucked into a submersible pump. Even if plants are not shredded by the koi, large-leafed plants such as lilies will act as perfect hiding places, preventing the koi from being seen easily.

Water depth – which aids body shape development – and volume in a koi pond are important considerations. After all, koi can grow to lengths above 60cm (2ft), and will do so in just a few years given the right conditions. Therefore, even a beginner's pond should be no less than, say, 13.5m cubic volume (3000gal). Ideally, depth should be 1.35m (4ft 6in) or more.

BUYING KOI

Most newcomers to the koi-keeping hobby are eager to improve their stock. Consequently they spend, or should spend, many happy hours in the company of fellow hobbyists, or with dealers, discussing, selecting and, ultimately, purchasing. This latter element can be expensive, particularly if the fish are brought home to inadequate facilities and eventually die. The new keeper will have learnt a salutary lesson in that the correct facilities, including an adequate filter, must be in place before buying commences.

It is best to purchase one, or at most two fish at a time, preferably separated by at least a couple of weeks to allow the filter system to adjust to the additional load. Daily water testing is the norm at these times (see 'Avoiding koi stress', page 135).

The quality of a koi is judged by factors such as skin quality, body shape, pattern and depth of coloration and the fish exhibiting the best of these

Facts & Figures 50

Keeping koi as a worldwide hobby – rather than as a home-grown one in Japan – only came about in the late 1960s, when transportation over large distances was made possible by the invention of the polythene bag.

Facts & Figures 51

Koi are poikilothermic animals – meaning that their body temperature takes up that of their surroundings. During the winter the body temperature of the koi falls along with the air and water temperature.

desirable characteristics are currently bred in Japan. Japan is not, however, the only producer of koi, and stocks from countries like Israel, Singapore, Korea, Thailand, the USA and the UK are improving rapidly.

If the pond-keeper wants to increase or improve koi stock, the country of origin should be taken into account as some places are very warm, with little or no winter. A koi's metabolism approaches its most efficient point at temperatures above 20°C (70°F); it follows, therefore, that during the winter – when the water temperature drops below 10°C (50°F) – the immune systems of our koi are not at their best for repelling the various pathogens that abound in our ponds. Furthermore, variable spring and autumn temperatures, that can cause swings of 5°C (40°F) or more overnight in small volumes of water, cause the koi to be stressed and maybe to succumb to disease or illness.

This single fact alone can cause losses in our koi ponds, particularly in springtime when the digestive systems of the fish stop and start on a regular basis. This is why the koi-keeping hobby is an all-year-round one requiring vigilance at all times.

IDENTIFICATION

Because Japan is the home of the koi, and this is where much of the breeding has taken place, koi are regularly referred to globally by their Japanese classes and variety names. The first thing to observe when trying to identify a class of koi is its scales. Does it have a metallic sheen? Metallic koi, because of their shiny, vivid coloration, really stand out in a pond, and are therefore often the first choice for beginners to the hobby. As koi-keeping skills are improved,

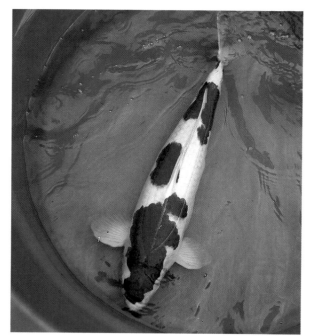

ABOVE: *A splendid example of a Kohaku – red markings on a white base*

RIGHT: *A Tancho Sanke has red and black markings on a white base*

then the more variable and arguably more interesting varieties are experimented with. These include the Go-Sanke varieties such as Tancho Sanke, Kohaku and Showa.

There are three classes of metallic koi varieties, and nine classes of non-metallic, with a further class for Kinginrin (fish having shiny scales of any body type). Each class contains varieties that are determined by variations of colour and pattern. The following is a simplified breakdown of the classification system (note that the distinction between one class and another can be blurred, and even experts are regularly baffled):

Facts & Figures 52

Don't refer to koi as 'koi carp'. The true name for koi is nishikigoi, which means 'brocaded carp'. The accepted contraction of nishikigoi is koi, but actually means 'carp'. Therefore to refer to koi as 'koi carp' is actually calling them 'brocaded carp carp'.

Metallic

HIKARIMONO: *single-coloured metallic koi often in gold, silver, yellow, orange, grey and platinum variations*

HIKARIMOYOMONO: *metallic orange or yellow on white*

HIKARIUTSURIMONO: *metallic forms of Utsuri and Showa Sanshoko koi (see below)*

Non-metallic

KOHAKU: *red markings on a white base*

TANCHO SANKE: *red and black markings on a white base*

SHOWA SANSHOKO: *red and white markings on a black base*

BEKKO: *black markings on a red, yellow or white base colour*

UTSURIMONO: *red, yellow or white markings on a black base colour*

ASAGI AND SHUSUI: *body blue or dark blue, with red/orange belly*

KOROMO: *red markings overlaid with darker pattering, on a white base colour*

TANCHO: *single red spot on the top of the head*

KAWARIMONO: *all other forms of non-metallic koi, including single colours*

It is vitally important that koi are fed with specially formulated koi food

AVOIDING KOI STRESS

I cannot emphasize too highly the importance of a stress-free environment for koi. Many factors make fish stressed, and the following five-point plan will alert you to the most severe:

1. **WASTE POLLUTANTS:** *these should be low, i.e. the water should be chemically clean. To achieve this, a biological filter of adequate size for the volume of fish population in the pond must be installed. Using a water-testing kit to ensure that the effect of fish respiration and waste have not made the water toxic by increased ammonia or nitrite levels is also essential. Basic kits can be purchased that test for ammonia, nitrite, nitrate and pH, but where koi keeping is concerned, testing for oxygen and carbonate hardness is important as well.*

2. **INSUFFICIENT VITAMINS AND MINERALS:** *supplement these by feeding with good quality food, specially formulated for koi.*

3. **LACK OF OXYGEN:** *koi need a good supply of oxygen. Water circulated via some form of water course helps aeration and will normally provide sufficient oxygen, but most koi keepers incorporate a venturi (a tube with a constriction to reduce or control fluid flow) or, preferably, an air pump into their system to provide the copious amount of oxygen required.*

4. **HEAVY METALS SUCH AS LEAD, COPPER AND ZINC:** *levels of these should be low or, better still, completely absent, as they can restrict growth, prevent reproduction and cause death if allowed to persist and accumulate in the koi's body. If a water quality report (normally free from your mains water supplier), shows these levels to be high in your incoming mains tap water, then an input water filter designed to remove these metals is advisable.*

5. **VARIABLE LEVELS OF TEMPERATURE:** *temperature stability is a parameter of water quality often overlooked, but variable levels can seriously affect the lives of the fish. Koi keepers often add some form of thermostatically controlled heating to their pond system to achieve stability of temperature, and swings can be minimized by creating and using during the winter months a removable cover made from an insulating material such as bubble plastic.*

As mentioned in Chapter 4, to enjoy a pond at its best the water should be clear, but the water clarity alone does not guarantee good water – indeed 'green' water has the benefit of developing the colours of koi. However, if the water is not clear, then viewing these beautiful fish is restricted.

CHAPTER 11

AMPHIBIOUS AND INSECTIVOROUS WILDLIFE

The wildlife that take up residence in and around your water garden can provide as much enjoyment and fascination as any other aspect of pond-keeping.

Amazingly, if you had the most barren of gardens, dug a hole in the ground and lined it, then filled it with water and left it there, within a couple of months it would be teeming with wildlife. Flying insects such as beetles and dragonflies would move in (even if the nearest breeding groups were over two miles away), and amphibian reptiles like frogs and toads would appear as if from nowhere. Miniscule creatures are often carried on the wind from one watery haven to another – so why shouldn't they land at yours?

So, if all this can happen naturally, why deliberately set out to attract wildlife to a pond? To answer this we must understand why it is so important to preserve our wildlife heritage. The natural habitats for aquatic and amphibious wildlife – woodland or moorland streams, natural springs, village ponds, marshlands, clean rivers, and so on – are disappearing as a result of changing agricultural and industrial land uses, new roads and spreading towns. This is exacerbated by the gradual climatic changes, which have caused many waterways – ponds and streams predominantly – to dry up. Therefore, if wildlife habitats are disappearing, then so is the wildlife itself.

A female azure damselfly at rest on a reed

Facts & Figures 53

The distinction between garden pests and garden wildlife is a fine one. In a perfectly balanced garden there should be a stable food chain of prey and predator. For example, destroying all of the greenfly in a garden will deprive ladybirds and bluetits of food. And a garden without any slugs at all is unlikely to have any frogs or toads (even if there is a pond). Low populations of most pests should be tolerated, and will help to encourage some of the forms of wildlife listed in this chapter.

In fact, domestic ponds do not always attract wildlife: formal pools, for example, which have straight sides, perhaps few plants, and maybe gushing fountains, will be fairly inhospitable places for insects and delicate aquatic creatures. So, too, will ponds that are geared up for crystal clear water, perhaps with sophisticated filters and UV clarifiers which can, of course, neutralize tiny creatures as well as unwanted algae.

Inviting wildlife to your pond, by making it a welcome place to inhabit, is a positive contribution to the threat. So, what can you do?

HELP TO ENCOURAGE WILDLIFE

We have already considered making a 'beach' (see Chapter 3), which is as much for encouraging wildlife as it is a decorative feature. Other things you can do to make your water garden attractive for wildlife include the following:

Don't
● have pools with steep sides, which make it difficult for animals to get out of the water.
● stock large populations of ornamental fish, which will devour small creatures and plants.
● in larger areas, where waterfowl are welcome, don't put the pond near to large trees which would interrupt the flight access of waterfowl.

Do
● have an area of rockery near to the pond which can offer sanctuary to amphibians, such as frogs, toads and newts.

Pond snails feed on decaying plant matter

Facts & Figures 54

Fossil records show that ancestors of our current-day damselflies and dragonflies were flying some 300 million years ago. These were huge insects with a wingspan of around 70cm (28in). The species with which we are more familiar first began to appear around 150 million years ago.

● create a central island within the pond, as a haven for small birds and insects.
● grow lush bog garden plants, with a good canopy of leaves, to give small creatures essential protection.
● create a deep part of the pond, at least 90cm (3ft), which is too deep for certain predators, and where water temperatures are stable.
● allow dead and decaying wood to become a feature of your wildlife pond; these places can support many types of insect, as well as fungi, mosses and lichens.
● (perhaps most important of all), create some sort of platform, or sitting area, where you can observe (and feed) the wildlife at close quarters. The more you appreciate wildlife, the more you are likely to want to attract it.

RICH DIVERSITY OF LIFE: THE GOODIES

The following are beneficial creatures, and are generally attracted to gardens by the presence of a pond:

DAMSELFLIES AND DRAGONFLIES: *beautiful creatures usually in bright reds or blues. The larvae live under the water (up to five years in the case of some dragonflies), feeding on small creatures passing by. They gradually climb out of the pond to eventually emerge as adults. Damselflies are slightly daintier versions of the dragonfly, but as you can get red and blue versions of both, identification by colour alone is not wise. Both insects are found naturally wherever there is a large body of water, but more usually in country areas rather than towns or cities.*

FRESHWATER SNAILS: *these will probably need to be introduced to your pond either by accident or design (they can be purchased from aquatic centres, or they*

Frogs are one of the gardener's most welcome visitors

may come in unwittingly with water plants). There are many different species of snail, some of which are tiny. Generally, snails are excellent at keeping ponds clean, as they feed on decaying plant matter and algae. The great pond snail also feeds on dead fish, soft-bodied invertebrates and even tadpoles. The flat ram's horn snail is particularly welcome as it feeds on algae and pondweed.

FROGS: these are possibly our most welcome visitors, roaming the garden devouring slugs and other

Tadpoles appear in spring

garden pests as they go. Sometimes heavy frog populations can 'bully' residential fish, but this does not often become a serious problem. Frogs usually have a smooth skin, varying in colour from deep olive green to a pale mustard yellow. Sometimes they have distinct brick red hues: these are usually old or sick frogs, and the reddish colour is an indication of the stresses their metabolism is undergoing. Adults spend most of the summer living in moist, shaded vegetation, but never far from the water. Frogs hibernate, and the males tend to take a deep breath before they sink to the bottom of the pond to dwell in the mud for two or three months. The females generally hide beneath piles of garden debris, to lie undisturbed for the winter period. From late winter, the frogs begin the familiar spawning rituals.

Facts & Figures 55

Toads have two raised lumps set behind their orange eyes. These lumps produce toxins, which make the toads unpalatable to predators.

Soon large glutinous clumps of eggs are seen, which turn into thousands upon thousands of agitated tadpoles within weeks. These feed on pond algae initially but, as they age, turn carnivore and eat small pond-dwelling invertebrates. Sadly for some tadpoles – which are, of course, small pond-dwelling invertebrates themselves – they will find that they are indeed food for their siblings. In other words, tadpoles are cannibals.

TOADS: *mainly night-time feeders; the most widely seen toads are the common and natterjack toads, which are usually larger, wartier and more 'rounded' than frogs. They are rarer than frogs, and can hibernate up to a mile away from the spawning pond, under piles of leaves, in holes in the soil, and in similar refuges. They will eat slugs, as well as caterpillars, beetles, woodlice and even ants. Toads arrive at the spawning pond in mid-spring and soon after, amongst the submerged weed, strings of eggs can be seen, wound around the plant stems. These eventually hatch as tadpoles, and the story from here is the same as for frogs.*

NEWTS: *smooth, crested and palmate newts are very shy, secretive creatures but they are just as beneficial as frogs and toads in eating garden pests. It is not easy to*

The common smooth newt

The palmate newt

The crested newt

identify between the newt species, as there are times of year when they can closely resemble one another. For example, smooth newts are the most common, and adult males can grow to 11cm (4½in) in length. They are dark brown and spotted, with a distinctive crest in the spring and summer, which can often confuse their appearance with crested newts. Palmate newts meanwhile are much smaller, but can be confused with smooth newts. Great crested newts (Trisures crisatus) is a protected species. Newts emerge from hibernation – generally from under pondside vegetation or large, flat stones – around mid-spring. Within a month they are engaged in an elaborate aquatic courtship, whereby the male moves around the female, waving his tail to give her his 'scent'. Eggs are laid individually, usually in submerged foliage.

Pond skaters spread their weight over the water

POND SKATERS: *there are ten species of pond skater – some will quickly fly in and inhabit a new pond, whilst those without wings must be carried to their new home on plants. These endearing insects are easily recognizable, because they 'walk' on the surface of the water, spreading their weight over as large an area as possible. They feed on dead and dying insects, and effectively 'clean-up' the surface of the water for us, albeit on a minuscule scale.*
WATER BOATMAN: *this familiar bug – actually a type of fly – swims just beneath the surface of the water,*

Facts & Figures 56

The medicinal leech – which doctors used to 'bleed' patients in times past – is one of the biggest species. An adult can be around 9cm (3½in) long when relaxed, and half as much again when extended.

using its legs and body like a boat being powered by oars. There are two main types: the lesser water boatman sieves organic matter from the water via hairs on its legs (it also uses its legs to rub together at mating time, rather like the grasshopper). The greater water boatman meanwhile is a predator, and can give we mere humans a painful bite.

RICH DIVERSITY OF LIFE: THE BADDIES

There are always a few unwelcome pond visitors as well, but fortunately they are not numerous. These are possibly the worst two:
LEECHES: *these must be the most unpopular of all pond inhabitants. They suck the bodily fluids out of their prey. To avoid getting leeches in your pond, check any plants or fish that you introduce – wherever they come from. Most species feed on water snails and fish.*
MOSQUITOES: *these prefer still waters to ponds with waterfalls and fountains, and will lay their eggs anywhere that is still, even in long-standing puddles and waterbutts. Fortunately the eggs and larvae are considered delicious by fish, so you will often find greater populations of mosquitoes where there is an absence of fish.*

Leech

Facts & Figures 57

Most water snails have tentacles that cannot be retracted in the way that land snails' tentacles can, and their eyes are at the base of the tentacles, not the tip, as most people imagine.

YEAR-ROUND MAINTENANCE GUIDE

CHAPTER 12

SEASON-BY-SEASON GUIDE

It is one thing to create a wonderful pond or water feature but, unless you are prepared to tend it and maintain it, there is very little point. Add to this the welfare of the fish, plants and wildlife that rely on the pond being kept in good condition, and you can see that a programme of regular activity is essential. Indeed, a monthly schedule – or seasonal schedule at the very least – is ideal. This chapter will set you on the right course.

EARLY WINTER

Preventing ice

Unless you live in a mild area, the water in your pond is likely to freeze over at some time during the winter, but there are precautions you can take to prevent this:

RUBBER BALLS: *some gardeners like to float a rubber ball in the pond. The theory is that the movement of the ball in the water, combined with the fact that the air within the ball is at a higher temperature than the water itself, prevents ice from forming within the vicinity. This is the cheapest method but, in reality, it very often fails to work at all, with the ball icing up and sticking fast. Also, it has to be said, a rubber ball on the surface of the water doesn't look particularly fetching.*

RUNNING WATER: *keep a section of the pond free from ice by running a fountain or waterfall permanently. The theory is that the moving water does not become still enough for ice to form. Without doubt this is the most successful method for keeping patches of pond surface ice-free. However, it is less effective in really severe winter cold, and of course there is a cost in terms of the electricity bill and wear and tear on the pump.*

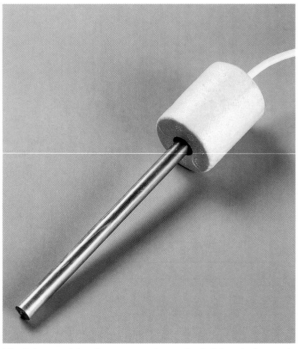

Electric pond heaters comprise a straight rod element and a float

ELECTRIC HEATERS: *if you have a power supply laid on for a pump, installing an electric pool heater becomes an easy and reliable option. It will usually comprise a straight rod element fitted through a wooden or polystyrene float which keeps the heater at surface level. It is plugged in directly to the mains supply and left in position whenever hard frost is forecast. Very effective, and not particularly expensive.*

If your pool has already iced over, you could try the following remedy:

BOILING PAN: *place a saucepan full of boiling water on the ice to melt a hole. If the ice is more than 1cm (½in) thick, and the saucepan is of average weight*

Using a pan of boiling water to create a hole in ice is a slow process

and thickness, it can take five minutes or more to melt the hole, so it is a bit like watching paint dry. To provide the pond with enough 'holes' to prevent the build-up of noxious gases in the water, can take several hours of to-ing and fro-ing with boiling pans. And the whole process needs to take place again the following day!

Never, ever, use a hammer, boot, screwdriver, elbow, or crowbar to break the ice. Although effective, the shockwaves and reverberation could stun or even kill the animal and fish life in your pond.

Create a fish sanctuary

If your pond is on the small side and has little greenery in winter, there may be nowhere for your fish to hide. This in itself will do them no harm, but it does mean that they have nowhere to dart if a heron or a cat appears. To create a sanctuary, you can cut some short lengths of black plastic pipe and gently drop them into the pool. They won't be obtrusive, but could make the difference between life and death for the fish.

Other water garden jobs for early winter

● Plan new ponds or water features
● Continue to remove blanketweed and other forms of algae
● Choose a mild, still day to pot on any pondside container plants that have outgrown their current pot
● Clear the pond of any autumn leaves that have fallen from nearby trees or shrubs
● Reflect on the year gone by and what might have gone wrong

What's looking good now in the garden?
WATER GARDEN & BOG PLANTS:
   Umbrella plant (Cyperus involucratus)
   Water hawthorn (Aponogeton distachyos)
   Various grasses, rushes and sedges
OTHER GARDEN FLOWERS:
   Crocus, cyclamen, eranthis, galanthus, helleborus, iris, leucojum, sternbergia and 'Universal' winter pansies

MID-WINTER

Check overwintering plants

Tender pond plants such as water hyacinth (eichhornia), that were lifted in autumn for storing indoors or under glass, should be inspected every two weeks or more during winter. The atmosphere and heat in which they are being kept will determine whether or not they need watering or misting – sometimes misting over the tops of the plants is all that they require. As the winter progresses, they will need checking more often for signs of life, and may need to be moved to a lighter or warmer position.

Fish

Many pond-keepers stop feeding their fish completely in winter, while others believe that if the weather is mild and the fish are active, their reserves will be depleted if they don't eat.

If the fish are swimming close to the surface, offer them a sprinkling of food. If they take it, give them a little more; if they decline, then stop.

Other water garden jobs for mid-winter

● All jobs as for early winter
● Weed the bog garden
● On mild days, plant new trees and shrubs along the water's edge, or in the bog garden
● Take care not to disturb hibernating wildlife

A mid-winter bloomer – Crocus vernus 'Pickwick'

What's looking good now in the garden?

WATER GARDEN & BOG PLANTS:

Umbrella plant (Cyperus involucratus)
Water hawthorn (Aponogeton distachyos)
Various grasses, rushes and sedges

OTHER GARDEN FLOWERS:

Anemone, chionodoxa, crocus, cyclamen, eranthis, erythronium, galanthus, helleborus, iris, saxifraga, scilla and 'Universal' winter pansies

If goldfish are taking a bit of food at this time of year, give them a little bit more

Late winter is the best time to dig out a new pond

LATE WINTER

Excavation work

If you are thinking about making a new pond, or re-shaping or enlarging an existing one, this is a good time to do it. If the work is completed now, you will be able to start planting, and introducing fish in about six weeks, which will bring you nicely in to the early to mid-spring season.

The most important thing to bear in mind is the depth of your proposed pond. It must be at least 45cm (18in) deep, and preferably 60cm (2ft) or more, and digging to this depth can be quite difficult. However it will be worth it, for it will provide an extra volume of water for plants to root and thrive, and for fish to flourish.

For serious excavation work, either hire a small digger, or hold a pond-digging party for all your able-bodied friends!

Wildlife

At this time of year frogs are mating, and there will be an abundance of frog spawn and tadpoles as a result. It is important to ensure that any frogs – as well toads and newts – can escape from the pond when the time is right. If the sides of your pond are vertical, or the edges overhang the water, install a small ramp, so that they can escape. A small log, or plank, if discreetly positioned, is ideal.

Large clumps of frogspawn will appear now

Other water garden jobs for late winter

● Add oxygenators to your pond
● Lift and divide overgrown marginals
● Give waterlilies in underwater planters a feed, by inserting tablets of fertilizer into the soil, next to the crown of the plant
● Top up water levels following the winter onslaught

What's looking good now in the garden?
WATER GARDEN & BOG PLANTS:
Drumstick primula (Primula denticulata)
Water hawthorn (Aponogeton distachyos)
OTHER GARDEN FLOWERS:
Anemone, chionodoxa, crocus, cyclamen, eranthis, erythronium, fritillaria, gentiana, hyacinthus, narcissus, primula, pulmonaria, saxifraga, scilla and tulipa

EARLY SPRING

Take out the debris

● Remove pond algae as and when you see it. It will only flourish if left unchecked, and will then become entangled with your more precious aquatic plants.

● Dead leaves should also be removed. Decaying vegetation will pollute the water and end up harming the fish. If you feel that a complete spring clean is necessary, a temporary home will need to be found for the fish.

Fish

Fish are cold-blooded, which means that they become more active as the temperature rises, and the fat reserves that sustained them during the winter will be exhausted now. With their resistance to infections at its lowest, fish need careful nurturing to restore their normal strength and energy and to improve their health generally in time for the breeding season. So, it's important to start feeding them, but don't use too much food or it will contaminate the water. Scatter a few pellets on the surface in the evening and add a few more if they take the first batch.

BELOW: *If you need to empty your pond for a spring clean, fish will need a temporary home.*
BELOW RIGHT: *Grape hyacinths* (Muscari armeniacum)

Other water garden jobs for early spring

● Plant new plants in the bog garden
● Following the winter, it is a good idea to test the quality and pH of the water, and make any remedial treatments
● Feed containerized aquatic plants with appropriate pellets, and established bog garden plants with general fertilizer, but do not allow any run-off to enter the pond
● Lift and divide overgrown marginals
● If you removed your submersible pump from the pond before the onset of winter (see Mid-autumn, page 156), now is the time to re-install it

What's looking good now in the garden?

WATER GARDEN & BOG PLANTS:
Arum italicum *'Marmoratum'*
Arum lily (Zantedeschia aethiopica)
Bugle (Ajuga reptans)
Cotton grass (Eriophorum angustifolium)
Drumstick primula (Primula denticulata)
Water hawthorn (Aponogeton distachyos)

OTHER GARDEN FLOWERS:
Anemone, bellis, brunnera, cheiranthus, chionodoxa, convallaria, crocus, cyclamen, erythronium, fritillaria, gentiana, hyacinthus, iris, leucojum, muscari, narcissus, polygonatum, primula, scilla and tulipa

Mid-spring is the ideal time to divide, tidy up and repot waterlilies

MID-SPRING

In the bog garden

● Give the plants a little extra food now, but always use fertilizers with caution near a pond. When there is no wind, sprinkle a handful of fish, blood and bone powder around the base of the plants, rather than spraying liquid feed over them.

● Stake any plants that are now putting on lush young growth at a fast rate. At this time of year it's best to use 'wrap-around' support, to avoid damaging the stems.

Fish

Watch your fish. At this time, as temperatures rise, fish begin to spawn. For several days the males will be seen pursuing and almost 'bullying' the females by chasing them into the denser patches of pondweed and it is there that the females will be stimulated to lay their tiny eggs.

Other water garden jobs for mid-spring

● Introduce new aquatic plants to your pond
● Divide overgrown waterlily clumps
● Watch for clusters of snails' eggs
● Rid your pond of algae and blanketweed – at this time it can be at its worst
● Check for signs of slugs on bog garden plants and marginals, and treat as appropriate

What's looking good now in the garden?

WATER GARDEN & BOG PLANTS:

Arum italicum 'Marmoratum'
Arum lily (Zantedeschia aethiopica)
Astilbes
Bog bean (Menyanthes trifoliata)
Bugle (Ajuga reptans)
Candelabra primula (Primula beesiana)
Candelabra primula (Primula japonica)
Candelabra primula (Primula pulverulenta)
Cotton grass (Eriophorum angustifolium)
Drumstick primula (Primula denticulata)
Globe flower (Trollius europaeus)
Golden club (Orontium aquaticum)
Greater spearwort (Ranunculus lingua 'Grandiflorus')
Japanese water iris (Iris laevigata)
Marsh marigold (Caltha palustris)
Skunk cabbage (Lysichiton americanus)
Water avens (Geum rivale)
Water forget-me-not (Myosotis scorpioides)
Water violet (Hottonia palustris)
Yellow flag iris (Iris pseudacorus)

OTHER GARDEN FLOWERS:

Allium, anemone, aquilegia, bellis, cheiranthus, convallaria, cyclamen, dicentra, erythronium, fritillaria, gentiana, hyacinthus, leucojum, muscari, narcissus, ornithogalum, papaver, polygonatum, saxifraga, trillium and tulipa

LATE SPRING

In the bog garden

● Now is a good time to tidy the bog garden and remove any dead or diseased foliage.

● Check to see if plants that flower in early or mid-spring are affected by mildew – just think of forget-me-nots. By cutting the affected parts hard back, you can encourage fresh new growth and perhaps a new crop of flowers later in the summer.

● Dead-heading is also important. Apart from making the plant less ugly it removes any areas where mould can set in. Never forget that by its nature a bog garden is damp all of the time and botrytis, grey mould and similar diseases may be more troublesome here than elsewhere in the garden.

● A well-made bog garden should be moist for most of the time, but in prolonged periods of hot, dry weather, the ground – and therefore the plants – can sometimes need extra help. In the evening, use a garden sprinkler to thoroughly

Hostas are looking good now. This is H. fortunei aurea

What's looking good now in the garden?

WATER GARDEN & BOG PLANTS:

Arum italicum *'Marmoratum'*
Arum lily (Zantedeschia aethiopica)
Bog arum (Calla palustris)
Bog bean (Menyanthes trifoliata)
Brass buttons (Cotula coronopifolia)
Bugle (Ajuga reptans)
Candelabra primula (Primula beesiana)
Candelabra primula (Primula japonica)
Candelabra primula (Primula pulverulenta)
Common water plantain (Alisma plantago)
Sweet flag (Acorus calamus)
Flowering rush (Butomus umbellatus)
Giant prickly rhubarb (Gunnera manicata)
Globe flower (Trollius europaeus)
Golden club (Orontium aquaticum)
Greater spearwort (Ranunculus lingua *'Grandiflorus'*)
Himalayan cowslip (Primula florindae)
Houttuynia cordata *'Chameleon'*

Marsh marigold (Caltha palustris)
Musk flower (Mimulus luteus)
Ornamental rhubarb (Rheum palmatum)
Riverside windflower (Anemone rivularis)
Rodgersia podophylla
Skunk cabbage (Lysichiton americanus)
Water avens (Geum rivale)
Water forget-me-not (Myosotis scorpioides)
Water violet (Hottonia palustris)
Various astilbe, hemerocallis, hostas and water irises

OTHER GARDEN FLOWERS:

Various bedding, including ageratum, begonia, pelargonium, godetia, impatiens, mesembryanthemum, nicotiana, tagetes and viola

Various herbaceous perennials and bulbs, including acanthus, allium, campanula, delphinium, dianthus, erigeron, geranium, gladiolus, lilium, lupinus, meconopsis, papaver, peonies, polygonatum, phlox and saxifraga

wet the area. A permanently installed trickle irrigation system would be an even better idea, as you would simply have to turn on the tap for a period of time.

Fish

⬤ If your pond fish have spawned, make sure that the fry have access to a shallow area, safe from the attentions of adult fish who will consider them as tasty morsels.

⬤ If the water has reached 15°C (70°F), you could transfer some of your tropical fish from indoor aquaria to the pond for the duration of the summer.

Other water garden jobs for late spring

⬤ All jobs as for mid-spring

⬤ Check for signs of plant pests, such as aphids, and treat as appropriate

⬤ Control the spread of duckweed, or your pond could be covered by the end of summer

EARLY SUMMER

Evaporation

After a few days of hot weather water gardeners everywhere are asking themselves if their ponds have sprung a leak. In most cases, they won't have but it's surprising how much water can be lost through evaporation on a really hot day. This is particularly important with small water features such as water barrels or wall-mounted fountains.

Not only does the pond look less attractive, but life begins to be pretty uncomfortable for the amphibia in it, too. It is, therefore, important to keep the water level topped up regularly. A fine-spray attachment on the end of a hose is ideal, otherwise the pool will be churned up and plants disturbed. If you have an open-ended hose, allow the water to trickle into the pond.

First, however, check that your local water company regulations allow you to use a hose in this way. Although hand-held hoses are generally

Top up water levels in ponds and small water features in hot weather

still acceptable, increasingly there is a requirement to have a water meter installed if you want to leave a hose unattended for any length of time.

Fish

In really hot weather, the water becomes comparatively warm and the fish can become lethargic. Feeding should be reduced slightly during the warmest periods.

Other water garden jobs for early summer

● All jobs as for late spring
● Check whether overgrown clumps of oxygenators and other fast-growing aquatics need to be thinned
● Weed the bog garden, and apply copious amounts of water during dry spells
● Check and prune waterlilies

The water forget-me-not (Myosotis scorpioides) *will flower throughout summer*

What's looking good now in the garden?

WATER GARDEN & BOG PLANTS:

Arrow arum (Peltandra undulata)
Arrowhead (Sagittaria sagittifolia)
Arum lily (Zantedeschia aethiopica)
Bog arum (Calla palustris)
Bog bean (Menyanthes trifoliata)
Branched bur-reed (Sparganium erectum)
Brass buttons (Cotula coronopifolia)
Candelabra primula (Primula beesiana)
Common water plantain (Alisma plantago)
Chinese loosestrife (Lysimachia clethroides)
Flowering rush (Butomus umbellatus)
Giant prickly rhubarb (Gunnera manicata)
Globe flower (Trollius europaeus)
Goat's beard (Aruncus dioicus)
Golden club (Orontium aquaticum)
Greater spearwort (Ranunculus lingua 'Grandiflorus')
Himalayan cowslip (Primula florindae)
Houttuynia cordata *'Chameleon'*
Lady's mantle (Alchemilla mollis)
Marsh marigold (Caltha palustris)
Musk flower (Mimulus luteus)

Ornamental rhubarb (Rheum palmatum)
Pickerel weed (Pontederia cordata)
Primula vialli
Purple monkey flower (Mimulus lewisii)
Ragged robin (Lychnis flos-cuculi)
Riverside windflower (Anemone rivularis)
Rodgersia aesculifolia
Skunk cabbage (Lysichiton americanus)
Sweet flag (Acorus calamus)
Water avens (Geum rivale)
Water forget-me-not (Myosotis scorpioides)
Water hawthorn (Aponogeton distachyos)
Water soldiers (Stratiotes aloides)
Water violet (Hottonia palustris)
Yellow pond lily (Nuphar lutea)
Various astilbe, hemerocallis, hosta, water irises and nymphaea (waterlily)

OTHER GARDEN FLOWERS:

Bedding as for late spring, with the addition of bedding antirrhinum, begonias, dahlias, lobelia, petunia, salvia and stocks
Herbaceous and bulbs as for late spring, with the addition of achillea, kniphofia, oenothera, spiraea, tropaeoloum and verbascum

Remove dead or damaged waterlily leaves before they rot and pollute the water

MID-SUMMER

Wish you were here...

For most people with families (and many others as well, of course), high summer is the time for the annual holiday. Life in the pond won't actually come to a grinding halt if you're not there to tend to its every need for a couple of weeks, but there are a few things you could do to maintain optimum performance of water, plants and fish:

● Ask a neighbour to switch on any aeration

Feeding blocks can be used to provide your fish with nourishment whilst you are away

device (i.e. a fountain or a waterfall/cascade) for a short while during the period you're away. This will help to oxygenate the water. If you don't have a powered aeration device, tell your neighbour that emptying a bucket of clean water, or running a hosepipe into the pond on thundery days will do some good.

● Make sure any water plant seedlings and young plants you're in the course of propagating are covered with enough water in their trays, and keep them out of the sun to reduce evaporation.

Fish

● As long as there are plenty of water plants of all kinds in your pond, fish can generally manage for a couple of weeks without supplementary feeding. Block feeders are available for fish in ponds that have few plants. These blocks mainly comprise calcium impregnated with specially formulated fish food pellets.

● Fish need oxygen, and the amount of oxygen in pond water decreases when the temperature rises. When the water temperature rises to 25°C (80°F) or higher, fish are likely to gulp air at the water's surface, or leave a bubbly froth in their wake. Oxygenating the water, as described above, will be important.

Other water garden jobs for mid-summer
● All jobs as for early summer
● Remove the faded flowers from early summer-flowering bog garden plants (such as hemerocallis)
● Pond levels may still need topping up in warm weather
● Continue to remove blanketweed and other forms of algae

RIGHT: *The variegated reed mace*
(Typha latifolia *'variegata'*)

What's looking good now in the garden?
WATER GARDEN & BOG PLANTS:
Arrowhead (Sagittaria sagittifolia)
Arum lily (Zantedeschia aethiopica)
Bog pimpernel (Anagallis tenella)
Branched bur-reed (Sparganium erectum)
Brass buttons (Cotula coronopifolia)
Chinese loosestrife (Lysimachia clethroides)
Common water plantain (Alisma plantago)
Filipendula camtschatica
Frogbit (Hydrocharis morsus-ranae)
Giant prickly rhubarb (Gunnera manicata)
Goat's beard (Aruncus dioicus)
Golden club (Orontium aquaticum)
Greater spearwort (Ranunculus lingua *'Grandiflorus'*)
Houttuynia cordata *'Chameleon'*
Lady's mantle (Alchemilla mollis)
Mare's tail (Hippuris vulgaris)
Marsh gentian (Gentiana pneumonanthe)
Marsh St John's wort (Hypericum elodioides)
Musk flower (Mimulus luteus)
Pickerel weed (Pontaderia cordata)
Purple monkey flower (Mimulus lewisii)
Ragged robin (Lychnis flos-cuculi)
Reed mace (Typha latifolia)
Rodgersia aesculifolia
Sweet flag (Acorus calamus)
Sweet galingale (Cyperus longus)
Water forget-me-not (Myosotis scorpioides)
Water fringe (Nymphoides peltatum)
Water hawthorn (Aponogeton distachyos)
Water hyacinth (Eichhornia crassipes)
Water mint (Mentha aquatica)
Water soldiers (Stratiotes aloides)
Water violet (Hottonia palustris)
Willow grass (Persicaria amphibia)
Yellow pond lily (Nuphar lutea)
Various astilbe, hemerocallis, hosta, water irises and nymphaea (waterlily)
OTHER GARDEN FLOWERS:
Various bedding including ageratum, alyssum, antirrhinum, begonia, godetia, impatiens, lathyrus, lobelia, mesembryanthemum, petunia, salvia and stocks
Various herbaceous and bulbs including acanthus, allium, dahlia, dianthus, echinacea, echinops, erigeron, gazania, geum, geranium, gladiolus, helenium, helianthus, helichrysum, kniphofia, lavatera, liatris, lilium, oenothera, papaver, penstemon, rudbeckia, tigridia, verbena and verbascum

LATE SUMMER

Tidy, tidy, tidy...

After the warm summer months when the pond has sustained itself without too much human assistance, there is now a steady increase in the number of jobs needing to be done.

Plants are starting to die down and the rate of decline is faster than the rate of growth, so late summer is the time to start a weekly routine of pulling out dead leaves and stems from your pond, before they sink to the bottom. If you do not remove them, they will give off harmful gases but, if kept to just small quantities, the gases can escape from the pond and do little harm. Large quantities however can pollute the water, and during winter the pond may freeze over, so that the potentially toxic gases would build up under the ice, and the fish suffer.

Your weekly tidying regime should be as follows:

⬤ Cut and clear away any collapsing stems and leaves before they enter the water.

What's looking good now in the garden?

WATER GARDEN & BOG PLANTS:

Arrowhead (Sagittaria sagittifolia)
Arum italicum 'Marmoratum'
Arum lily (Zantedeschia aethiopica)
Branched bur-reed (Sparganium erectum)
Brass buttons (Cotula coronopifolia)
Cardinal flower (Lobelia cardinalis)
Chinese loosestrife (Lysimachia clethroides)
Common water plantain (Alisma plantago)
Flowering rush (Butomus umbellatus)
Frogbit (Hydrocharis morsus-ranae)
Golden rays (Ligularia dentata)
Greater spearwort (Ranunculus lingua *'Grandiflorus'*)
Hemp agrimony (Eupatorium cannabinum)
Houttuynia cordata *'Chameleon'*
Kirengeshoma palmata
Lady's mantle (Alchemilla mollis)
Lavender musk (Mimulus ringens)
Mare's tail (Hippuris vulgaris)
Marsh gentian (Gentiana pneumonanthe)
Marsh St John's wort (Hypericum elodioides)
Meadowsweet (Filipendula ulmaria)
Pickerel weed (Pontaderia cordata)
Purple monkey flower (Mimulus lewisii)
Reed mace (Typha latifolia)
Sweet flag (Acorus calamus)
Water hawthorn (Aponogeton distachyos)
Water hyacinth (Eichhornia crassipes)
Water mint (Mentha aquatica)
Water fringe (Nymphoides peltatum)
Water soldiers (Stratiotes aloides)
Willow grass (Persicaria amphibia)
Yellow pond lily (Nuphar lutea)

OTHER GARDEN FLOWERS:

Achillea, aconitum, agapanthus, Anemone *x* hybrida, *arctotis, aster (Michaelmas daisy), canna, chrysanthemum, colchicum, crinum, cyclamen, dahlia, echinops, erigeron, felicia, gazania, gladiolus, autumn gentian, geranium, helianthus, impatiens, ipomoea, kniphofia, lavatera, liatris, mesembryanthemum, monarda, nicotiana, penstemon, phlox, physostegia, rudbeckia, schizostylus, sedum, solidago and verbena*

LEFT: Dead-head all perennial and bog garden plants – here faded hemerocallis blooms are being removed

● Trim back fading marginal plants by two-thirds (but don't cut them too low in case their hollow stems become totally submerged and rot).

● Leave one or two areas as cover for the various water animals that like to spend their winter in hiding near the banks.

● The older leaves of waterlilies will be looking increasingly ragged now. Pull these away, or cut them with a sharp knife. If the ragged leaves are just out of normal reach, attach a razor blade to a cane. It'll make a fine cutting tool.

● Keep an eye out for the two main waterlily pests: aphids and lily beetle. The aphids (blackfly and greenfly) are instantly recognizable. The beetles are brown and small (as beetles go). You will see the damage created by the beetles: they nibble at the leaves causing holes in and on the edges of the leaves. Fire a jet of water at the leaves to knock the pests in to the water, and remove the worst affected leaves.

Fish

Fish need oxygen, and the amount of oxygen in pond water decreases when the temperature rises. When the water level rises to 25°C (80°F) or higher, fish are likely to gulp air at the water's surface, or leave a bubbly froth in their wake. Running a fountain or waterfall will help to oxygenate the water, or failing that simply agitate a jet of water from a hosepipe for a few minutes.

Other water garden jobs for late summer

● As daylight lengths shorten, thin floating plants (such as duckweed and azolla) to allow as much sunlight on to the pond as possible

● Divide overgrown marginal plants before the soil and water are too cold for replanting

● Detach young portions of tender aquatic plants (such as the water hyacinth, eichhornia) for overwintering safely indoors

● Tropical or tender fish that have been enjoying the summer outdoors should be returned to their winter quarters indoors, particularly if the water temperature falls below 15°C (60°F)

RIGHT: Fish need oxygen, and running a waterfall, or fountain, will help to oxygenate the water

EARLY AUTUMN

The great divide

Perennial plants in the bog garden can be lifted and divided both in spring and autumn, and now is as good a time to tackle all but the most tender perennials, which are better left until spring.

Water and waterside plants tend to be more vigorous than their drier garden counterparts which means that you need to divide them rather more frequently – pull apart large clumps and discard the tough older centres, replanting only the more vigorous, outer sections.

Don't be tempted to lift waterlilies and other fully aquatic species now – they should be left until spring.

Marginal cut-backs

Many clumps of marginal species will have spent the summer trying to march their way across the pond and reclaim the open water. They must now be cut back.

Whereas perennial plants in dry soil should be cut back to just above ground level, it's best to leave marginal species with rather longer stumps, especially if they are a trifle tender and have hollow stems; otherwise the accumulation of water within the stem bases – which will freeze during winter – can cause damage and allow rot to penetrate the crown.

Fish

It is now that fish need to build up their food reserves. Being cold-blooded, they will be fairly inactive during the depths of winter, and their survival will depend on what they have eaten during summer and autumn.

Continue to feed them regularly, but it is even more important from now on that you make sure they eat all that is given to them. Excess food will drop to the bottom and rot, so scatter a few flakes or pellets and supply more only if the first are completely devoured.

Other water garden jobs for early autumn

● Continue to remove blanketweed and other forms of algae

● As daylight lengths shorten, thin floating plants (such as duckweed and azolla) to allow as much sunlight on to the pond as possible

● Scoop out from the pond any fallen leaves or rotting plant material

● Detach young portions of tender aquatic plants (such as eichhornia and pistia, the water lettuce) for overwintering safely indoors

● Last chance to return to their winter quarters indoors any tropical or tender fish that have been outside during the summer, particularly if the water temperature falls below 15°C (60°F)

What's looking good now in the garden?
WATER GARDEN & BOG PLANTS:

Arum italicum *'Marmoratum'*
Bladderwort (Utricularia vulgaris)
Bugbane (Cimicifuga simplex)
Brass buttons (Cotula coronopifolia)
Cardinal flower (Lobelia cardinalis)
Greater spearwort (Ranunculus lingua *'Grandiflorus'*)
Marsh St John's wort (Hypericum elodioides)
Pickerel weed (Pontaderia cordata)
Purple monkey flower (Mimulus lewisii)
Reed mace (Typha latifolia)
Umbrella plant (Cyperus involucratus)
Water fringe (Nymphoides peltatum)
Water hawthorn (Aponogeton distachyos)
Water hyacinth (Eichhornia crassipes)
Willow grass (Persicaria amphibia)

OTHER GARDEN FLOWERS:

Aconitum, anemone, aster, ceratostigma, chrysanthemum, colchicum, cortaderia, crocus, cyclamen, gaillardia, galanthus, gentiana, geum, helianthus, kniphofia, liriope, nerine, penstemon, rudbeckia, sedum, solidago, sternbergia, stokesia and verbena

Water lettuce (Pistia stratiotes) *needs to be overwintered in a frost-free environment*

MID-AUTUMN

Pump care

Most owners of ponds with moving water have submersible pumps, and there is a school of thought which proclaims that these should not only be left in the water all year round, but that they should also be working, pumping round the water 24 hours a day, 365 days a year.

During really cold weather the water movement, or 'agitation', that these pumps provide ensures that the pool has at least a small area free from ice.

Mid-autumn is the right time to disconnect and clean submersible pumps

Small bulbs look good when planted near to water – plant them during autumn

If you prefer to remove the pump and store it over winter, then now is the time to disconnect it. Clean it out as best you can, as well as the associated pipework. Surface pumps, in any case, will need to be so treated at this time.

Leaf collection

Continue to remove leaves from the pond or water feature. As autumn progresses, the greater the likelihood that ignored leaves will sink to the bottom of the pond, so be prepared to delve into the depths with your net or, even better, your hand. Try not to disturb the mud too much, as many creatures will be hibernating in it.

Spring bulbs

Small bulbs look extremely attractive when planted close to water, and this is the latest time to plant them if you want flowers next spring. Smaller narcissi, crocuses, snowdrops, muscari and scillas are particularly effective – avoid the larger varieties of bulbs (daffodils, tulips and hyacinths particularly) as they look inappropriate in this situation.

If your pool is formal, then the bulbs are best planted in containers (but do ensure that the new pots you're using are guaranteed to be frost-proof). If your pond is informal, then the bulbs are best planted into nearby beds – although not directly into a bog garden, where they are likely to rot.

Container plants

Growing perennial plants, as well as trees and shrubs, in containers close to more formal pools

---

What's looking good now in the garden?

WATER GARDEN & BOG PLANTS:

Purple monkey flower (Mimulus lewisii)
Royal fern (Osmunda regalis)
Umbrella plant (Cyperus involucratus)
Water hawthorn (Aponogeton distachyos)
Willow grass (Persicaria amphibia)
Various grasses, rushes and sedges

OTHER GARDEN FLOWERS:

Aconitum, anemone, aster, ceratostigma, chrysanthemum, colchicum, cortaderia, crocus, cyclamen, galanthus, gentiana, helenium, rudbeckia, schizostylis, sedum and sternbergia

Old gunnera leaves are ideal for covering the crowns of plants over the winter

makes a great deal of sense – you can't, after all, plant into paving stones! If the weather is still fairly mild, as it often is at this time of year, there is no harm in repotting some of the bigger specimens into slightly larger containers now.

Other water garden jobs for mid-autumn

● Continue to remove blanketweed and other forms of algae

● As daylight shortens, thin floating plants (such as duckweed and azolla) to allow as much sunlight on to the pond as possible

● Last chance to cover and protect any tender marginal or bog garden plants before the worst of the weather sets in

● Take hardwood cuttings of pondside trees and shrubs

LATE AUTUMN
Prepare for the future

This is a good time to start a new pond (or extend existing ones), free from the urgency of spring, the heat and dryness of summer and the cold and inhospitable ground conditions of winter. The weather now is usually warm enough to make the work pleasant, while the risk of prolonged frost is still slight.

If you are contemplating a new pond, before any practical work is carried out you must decide on its location. Remember the golden rules for pond positioning:

● Do place ponds in full sun
● Do place ponds on level sites
● Do not place ponds under trees
● Do not place ponds at the foots of slopes

Fish

Around now the water in the pond will reach 5°C (40°F), the critical point below which all feeding of fish should stop.

Other water garden jobs for late autumn

● All jobs as for mid-autumn
● Check your liner (or concrete) above the waterline for cracks and leaks
● Check for slippery paths and paving stones around the edge of the pond – these can be lethal
● Prevent ice forming (see Early Winter, page 142)
● Reflect on the year gone by and what might have gone wrong

What's looking good now in the garden?
WATER GARDEN & BOG PLANTS:
Royal fern (Osmunda regalis)
Umbrella plant (Cyperus involucratus)
Water hawthorn (Aponogeton distachyos)
Various grasses, rushes and sedges
OTHER GARDEN FLOWERS:
Autumn crocus, cyclamen, galanthus, helleborus, Iris unguicularis, schizostylis and sternbergia

---

LEFT: The umbrella plant (Cyperus involucratus) *is a marginal which sends up green floral 'rays' on arching stems 1m (3ft) high*

PROBLEM-SOLVING

CHAPTER 13

FREQUENTLY ASKED QUESTIONS

I hope that in this book I have covered all of the major subjects of interest to novice water gardeners, as well as to the more experienced pond-keeper. There are, however, a few points I have not covered specifically in the body of the book, and this chapter deals with those.

The following are the answers to the top ten questions I am asked most frequently:

1. FISH NOT EATING

Q

My pond fish do not eat during excessively hot or thundery weather. Is this natural, and should I stop feeding them at these times?

A

The reason your fish do not feed in hot or sultry weather is because there is not enough

Koi and pond fish feed only when climatic and atmospheric conditions are right

Moving koi from one pond to another is not an easy task

oxygen in the pond water. In climatic conditions like this, atmospheric oxygen becomes rather less abundant, and therefore harder to dissolve in water.

Too much growth of oxygenating plants, or nuisance algae such as green water and blanketweed, can actually lead to low oxygen levels in the water during the summer. Plants compete more successfully for available oxygen than fish, and very commonly the largest fish are found dead in the morning as a result of the overnight oxygen crash.

The digestion of food consumes vast amounts of oxygen, so the easiest way to tackle this problem is not to feed.

Even better though is to continue feeding, but instead consider some way of aerating your pond. It is important to keep pumps, waterfalls or fountains running continuously at these times to ensure the pond water is adequately aerated. If you want to save cash by running the pump for only 12 hours a day, turn it off at night. In hot and sultry weather reduce the food offered, removing uneaten food as it will consume vital oxygen as it decomposes.

2. MOVING KOI

Q

I have about a dozen koi and am planning to move house. I am concerned about moving them safely. Can you advise?

A

Preparing a pond at the new location is not always possible in advance of the actual day of the move, and so unless it is practical to keep the koi in the existing pond until the new pond is ready, you will need to find temporary accommodation for them.

Generally, joining a koi club can be of benefit to people even if they decide against continuing the hobby in their new home. Often established club members can help at these times by housing some if not all of a collection in their quarantine ponds. If for any reason you decide to give the hobby up, there are often club members who want to increase the size of their collections and may be able to give a good home to some of the unwanted koi.

Find out if there are any koi clubs in your new area, and start from there.

3. SHEET WATERFALL

Q

I want to create a waterfall in the style of a falling 'sheet' of water. What is the best method to make this?

A

Make a 'tray', either from lead, or anodised aluminium which has a downturned edge, off which water can fall as a curtain. It should be possible to bond this tray into the aperture using plenty of exterior mastic, so that water flows over the tray and not beneath it.

If you plan to use a submersible pump, remember that it should be housed in a generous reservoir at the lowest point of the whole system. A stream may not satisfy this requirement.

A sheet waterfall requires a sturdy pump and a level 'tray' with a downturned edge

4. LACKING WILDLIFE

Q

I have two ponds: one for fish, and the other for frog and tadpole spawn, and newt eggs, as I understand that keeping these away from the fish will increase the success rate. So why do I have so few adult frogs, toads and newts?

A

If most of the spawn and eggs develop into tadpoles successfully, and it is only when the live young are emerging that they seem to disappear, this could be due to a lack of food in the spawning pond. If there are few plants and little natural life for the tadpoles to feed on, it is crucial to supply daily doses of pelleted or flaked fish food, and maybe live foods like water-fleas (daphnia) a couple of times a week.

Once the tadpoles develop limbs and emerge into young adults, they need to get out of the water at regular intervals. Perhaps there are no easy exit routes for them: if the pond has vertical or near-vertical sides, then you need to position stones or bricks for the small creatures to climb up on.

Toads and frogs tend to emerge from the pond in a continuous flow, lasting several weeks and they can fall victim to a wide range of disasters at this time. There are, of course, many predators: natural ones like blackbirds, thrushes and herons, and domestic ones like the cat.

The only realistic way to offer protection to these baby amphibians is to let the vicinity around the pond go wild, which is unfortunate for the gardener wanting an ornamental, 'manicured' garden. If you have a small garden, then you'll need to let practically all of it go in this way.

The peak time for emergence varies according to location, climate and a whole host of other ecological and environmental factors, but as it draws near in your garden, allow the vegetation around the pond edges to grow long.

The lawn affords much protection to these creatures, but it can also be their downfall. Mowing the grass is actually one of the greatest killers of small amphibians. If you really have to mow when emergence is high, check the lawn thoroughly immediately beforehand.

A pond that stinks also looks unsightly, and should be drained and refilled

5. STINKING WATER

Q

I can't go near our pond as the smell of rotting matter is too great. What can I do?

A

Organic matter accumulates at the bottom of every pond – leaves fallen from surrounding plants, aquatic plants that have died down, fish waste, and dead and decaying organisms. This all gives rise to the ooze at the bottom, often referred to as silt. It is, effectively, a rich, thick mud.

The lack of oxygen in the sediment promotes the growth of certain bacteria which produce noxious gases such as hydrogen sulphide – which smells of bad eggs – and methane. A covering of ice in the winter, which prevents both oxygen getting in to the water, and gases from escaping, can make the pond even smellier.

Probably the best thing to do is drain the pond, extract the silt and refill it with clean water.

In future, make sure that the pond has plenty of oxygenating plants, and moving water, so that oxygen is continually being fed into the water.

6. GREEN WATER

Q

The water in my pond is like pea soup and pondweeds do not seem able to grow. What should I do?

A

This is the effect caused by millions of microscopic plants in suspension, which are present because of an imbalance of nutrients in the water. Fish are quite likely the culprits – their waste has produced both ammonia and phosphate.

Barley straw is often recommended in such situations, but it is not always the best solution. The process relies on the growth of beneficial bacteria and fungi on the straw. In theory, as these grow they produce a chemical which halts the growth of the algae – but this only works if the pond is well aerated. In stagnant ponds, the straw simply decays, so lowering the oxygen level even further.

The real solution lies in installing an ultra-violet filter and pump. Passing the green water under the UV lamp within the filter kills the algal cells, and returns cleaner water to the pond.

7. LEAKING CONCRETE POND

Q

I have an old concrete pond and there are cracks in it. I have to top up the water practically every day. What is the best course of action?

A

Set up an alternative temporary pond system to house your plants, fish and so on – a children's paddling pool can make a cheap and convenient emergency pond, but make sure you keep it away from predatory cats or herons.

To trace the leak from the concrete pond, let the water settle (turn off all pumps and filters), and allow the water to drop to the level at which it is escaping. The leak may be in the rendering – caused by excessive exposure to sunlight or general wear and tear. Alternatively it may be in the base concrete, due to outside influences such as plant roots growing through it.

A small leak can be repaired with an application of rendering but, where the leak is more serious, you may have to install a butyl liner as a membrane to maintain the water in the pond. Remember, if roots have caused the problem these will need treating before the liner is put in place. If not, they will continue to grow, and will damage the liner, causing the leak to start all over again.

Concrete ponds with serious leaks should be lined with butyl sheeting

8. NON-FLOWERING WATERLILIES

Q

Why do my waterlilies produce one or two flowers (if I'm lucky), when my neighbour's plants flower all summer long?

A

There are at least five different reasons why waterlilies are failing to flower well, and they are all fairly unrelated.

⬤ The condition of the water can play a great part. If you have quite a few fish, and perhaps not too many plants, there could be an excess of ammonia in the water, which can inhibit waterlily growth and flowering.

⬤ Perhaps your variety(ies) are unsuitable for the depth of pond. There are essentially two types of waterlily: those that prefer shallow water, and those that prefer deep water, (see pages 71–5 for more information on suitable varieties for given water depths).

⬤ An overcrowded plant can produce more leaf for survival than flower. You can tell if this is the case because the pads of the lily become curled and congested: normally they should be able to lie flat on the surface of the water.

⬤ Waterlilies dislike being placed too close to the splashes from a fountain or waterfall: the constant movement of water can inhibit flowering.

⬤ Waterlily flower buds can also provide tasty food for some fish, particularly koi or ghost carp.

It is important to remove as much blanketweed as possible by hand

There are fertilizers available from garden centres and shops that are specially formulated for waterlilies, and they should be added directly to the soil in the basket each spring.

9. BLANKETWEED/SILKWEED

Q

How do I get rid of this menace? It is tangled up in all my aquatic plants.

A

This is a form of algae characterized by long, fibrous strands which grow at a fast rate during the warmer months. The condition of the water can be largely responsible for the persistent growth of blanketweed (in much the same way as for the problem of green water – see Question 6).

In the short term it is important to remove as much of the weed as possible, using twist forks or rakes, or even stout wooden canes in the water to wind on the strands of weed and lift them out of the pond.

UV filters do not control blanketweed because it is filamentous but various chemical treatments will control its growth. Because the weed is sensitive to changes in day length and begins to grow fairly early in the year, such chemical treatment must be started in late winter or early spring.

Watercress starts growing at the same time of the year as blanketweed and, in a pond with a waterfall, can be grown successfully to compete

with the latter for available nutrients. The cress will need to be pruned back periodically, otherwise it will become a nuisance, too. (Note that watercress growing in fishpond water is not suitable for human consumption.)

10. BLACKFLY PROBLEM

Q

Most summers my waterlilies, and some other pond plants, are infested with clouds of small black flies. I don't want to spray chemicals, because they will get in to the pond. What can I do?

A

Waterlily aphids are almost certainly the pest in question. The only thing you can do, once the plants are infested, is to spray the leaves, forcefully, with a jet of water to wash the flies into the pond where, with luck, the fish will eat them.

Because these aphids lay their overwintering eggs on cherry and plum trees, it is easier to break their life cycle there rather than in the pond. Eggs laid in the cracks in the bark can be destroyed by spraying the tree with a tar oil winter wash, which is widely used on fruit trees during the dormant period to control a wide range of overwintering pests. If you spray thoroughly, you should find you have far fewer aphids the following year.

INDEX

Page numbers in **bold** refer to illustrations

TITLES AVAILABLE FROM
GMC Publications

BOOKS

Gardening

Alpine Gardening	Chris & Valerie Wheeler
Auriculas for Everyone: How to Grow and Show Perfect Plants	
	Mary Robinson
Beginners' Guide to Herb Gardening	Yvonne Cuthbertson
Beginners' Guide to Water Gardening	Graham Clarke
The Birdwatcher's Garden	Hazel & Pamela Johnson
Companions to Clematis: Growing Clematis with Other Plants	
	Marigold Badcock
Creating Contrast with Dark Plants	Freya Martin
Creating Small Habitats for Wildlife in your Garden	Josie Briggs
Exotics are Easy	GMC Publications
Gardening with Hebes	Chris & Valerie Wheeler
Gardening with Wild Plants	Julian Slatcher
Growing Cacti and Other Succulents in the Conservatory and Indoors	
	Shirley-Anne Bell
Growing Cacti and Other Succulents in the Garden	Shirley-Anne Bell
Growing Successful Orchids in the Greenhouse and Conservatory	
	Mark Isaac-Williams
Hardy Palms and Palm-Like Plants	Martyn Graham
Hardy Perennials: A Beginner's Guide	Eric Sawford
Hedges: Creating Screens and Edges	Averil Bedrich
Marginal Plants	Bernard Sleeman
Orchids are Easy: A Beginner's Guide to their Care and Cultivation	
	Tom Gilland
Plant Alert: A Garden Guide for Parents	Catherine Collins
Planting Plans for Your Garden	Jenny Shukman
Sink and Container Gardening Using Dwarf Hardy Plants	
	Chris & Valerie Wheeler
The Successful Conservatory and Growing Exotic Plants	Joan Phelan
Tropical Garden Style with Hardy Plants	Alan Hemsley
Water Garden Projects: From Groundwork to Planting	
	Roger Sweetinburgh

Photography

Close-Up on Insects	Robert Thompson
Double Vision	Chris Weston & Nigel Hicks
An Essential Guide to Bird Photography	Steve Young
Field Guide to Bird Photography	Steve Young
Field Guide to Landscape Photography	Peter Watson
How to Photograph Pets	Nick Ridley
In my Mind's Eye: Seeing in Black and White	Charlie Waite
Life in the Wild: A Photographer's Year	Andy Rouse
Light in the Landscape: A Photographer's Year	Peter Watson
Outdoor Photography Portfolio	GMC Publications
Photographing Fungi in the Field	George McCarthy
Photography for the Naturalist	Mark Lucock
Professional Landscape and Environmental Photography:	
From 35mm to Large Format	Mark Lucock
Rangefinder	Roger Hicks & Frances Schultz
Viewpoints from Outdoor Photography	GMC Publications
Where and How to Photograph Wildlife	Peter Evans

Art Techniques

Oil Paintings from your Garden: A Guide for Beginners	Rachel Shirley

VIDEOS

Drop-in and Pinstuffed Seats	David James
Stuffover Upholstery	David James
Elliptical Turning	David Springett
Woodturning Wizardry	David Springett
Turning Between Centres: The Basics	Dennis White
Turning Bowls	Dennis White
Boxes, Goblets and Screw Threads	Dennis White
Novelties and Projects	Dennis White
Classic Profiles	Dennis White
Twists and Advanced Turning	Dennis White
Sharpening the Professional Way	Jim Kingshott
Sharpening Turning & Carving Tools	Jim Kingshott
Bowl Turning	John Jordan
Hollow Turning	John Jordan
Woodturning: A Foundation Course	Keith Rowley
Carving a Figure: The Female Form	Ray Gonzalez
The Router: A Beginner's Guide	Alan Goodsell
The Scroll Saw: A Beginner's Guide	John Burke

MAGAZINES

Woodturning ◆ Woodcarving ◆ Furniture & Cabinetmaking
The Router ◆ New Woodworking
The Dolls' House Magazine
Outdoor Photography ◆ Black & White Photography ◆ Travel Photography
Machine Knitting News ◆ BusinessMatters

The above represents a selection of the titles currently published or scheduled to be published.
All are available direct from the Publishers or through bookshops, newsagents and specialist retailers.
To place an order, or to obtain a complete catalogue, contact:
GMC Publications,
Castle Place, 166 High Street, Lewes, East Sussex BN7 1XU United Kingdom
Tel: 01273 488005 Fax: 01273 478606
E-mail: pubs@thegmcgroup.com
Orders by credit card are accepted